Python Web Scraping: Collect and Analyze Data with BeautifulSoup

A Comprehensive Guide to Web Scraping Using Python

MIGUEL FARMER

RAFAEL SANDERS

Table of Content

TABLE OF CONTENTS

INTRODUCTION

Python Web Scraping: Collect and Analyze Data with BeautifulSoup

In an increasingly digital world, data has become the cornerstone of informed decision-making, business intelligence, and even personal insight. Whether it's scraping product prices from e-commerce sites, collecting news articles, or analyzing social media sentiment, web scraping offers a way to unlock vast amounts of information that can otherwise remain hidden behind the walls of complex websites. But to tap into this wealth of data, one must first master the art and science of web scraping—a process that is as essential as it is challenging.

Welcome to *Python Web Scraping: Collect and Analyze Data with BeautifulSoup*. This book aims to guide you through the process of collecting, analyzing, and storing data from the web, using one of the most powerful and popular tools available: Python. Python's flexibility, ease of use, and extensive libraries make it the ideal language for web scraping tasks, and BeautifulSoup, a library designed for quick HTML and XML parsing, is at the heart of this journey.

Whether you're a beginner just getting started or an expert looking to fine-tune your scraping techniques, this book has something to offer. Our goal is to help you understand the theory behind web scraping while also providing you with practical, real-world examples that can be immediately applied. Along the way, we'll explore not only the basics of web scraping but also how to handle complex data, automate your scraping processes, and work around the roadblocks that can often slow you down—like CAPTCHAs, rate-limiting, and scraping dynamic content. The techniques covered will ensure that your scraping projects are efficient, ethical, and legally sound.

What You Will Learn

1. **Core Web Scraping Techniques**
   We'll start with the essentials: setting up your Python environment, installing key libraries like BeautifulSoup and Requests, and learning how to navigate web pages by understanding HTML structures. From there, we'll progress through

selecting specific elements from web pages, handling dynamic content, and scraping multiple pages of a website.

2. **Data Handling and Analysis**
Once you have the data, we'll dive deep into how to process, clean, and analyze it. You'll learn how to store your scraped data in formats like CSV, JSON, or even databases, and how to manipulate and analyze the data using Python's powerful data analysis tools like Pandas and NumPy.

3. **Advanced Techniques and Automation**
For those looking to take their skills to the next level, we'll cover advanced topics like handling JavaScript content with Selenium, scraping large datasets using multithreading, and automating your scrapers to run on a schedule. You'll also learn how to build more robust and error-resistant scrapers that can handle complex, dynamic websites.

4. **Ethics and Legalities of Web Scraping**
Web scraping can often walk a fine line between legitimate use and legal violations. This book will address how to respect website terms of service, handle rate limits, and comply with legal guidelines,

ensuring that your scraping practices are both ethical and responsible.

5. **Real-World Case Studies**

Throughout this book, you'll encounter real-world case studies and examples designed to help you understand how to apply what you've learned in practical, everyday situations. From scraping e-commerce sites for price comparisons to collecting news articles for sentiment analysis, these examples will give you the hands-on experience needed to build your own web scraping projects.

Who Should Read This Book?

This book is designed for a wide audience, whether you're a complete beginner, a student of data science, or a professional seeking to expand your skill set in web scraping. If you've never written a web scraper before, don't worry—we'll guide you through each step with clear explanations and straightforward examples. However, even if you're already familiar with the basics, you'll find plenty of advanced techniques and best practices to help you refine your skills.

A Note on Practicality and Real-World Applications

This book isn't just about theory—it's about doing. You'll be encouraged to build real scrapers, tackle real-world problems, and handle data from actual websites. By the end of the book, you won't just know how to scrape data—you'll have the experience and confidence to take on any web scraping project that comes your way.

The Future of Web Scraping

The landscape of web scraping is ever-evolving. With new anti-scraping technologies being developed and new use cases constantly emerging, it's important to keep up with the times. This book not only teaches you the current methods and techniques for web scraping but also prepares you to adapt to the future of data collection.

Whether you're looking to scrape data for research, business analysis, or simply for learning purposes, this book will equip you with the tools you need to gather and analyze web data effectively, responsibly, and efficiently. Let's get started with understanding the basics, and soon you'll be scraping like a pro.

This introduction establishes the practical nature of the book, while outlining both beginner and advanced-level content, and setting the stage for the rest of the chapters. Would you like me to dive deeper into any of the topics covered here?

CHAPTER 1:

INTRODUCTION TO WEB SCRAPING AND PYTHON

Overview of Web Scraping

In the modern world, data is a goldmine, and much of it is scattered across various websites. Web scraping refers to the process of extracting this data from websites in an automated manner. Essentially, it's a way to "scrape" valuable content like text, images, or product information from web pages and convert it into structured data for analysis or further use.

The process typically involves sending HTTP requests to a website, downloading its HTML content, and then parsing that HTML to extract specific pieces of data. Web scraping is widely used for a variety of purposes, including competitive analysis, market research, data collection for research projects, and even personal use like aggregating news articles or tracking product prices.

Despite its power, web scraping isn't always straightforward. Websites are designed to be visually appealing and user-friendly, but scraping them often requires a deeper understanding of HTML, CSS, and how web pages are structured. This book aims

14

to help you gain that understanding, along with the tools necessary to extract data from almost any web page.

Ethical Considerations and Legal Concerns

While web scraping can be incredibly useful, it's important to remember that scraping isn't always legal or ethically sound. Many websites place restrictions on scraping through their terms of service (TOS), and failing to comply with those restrictions can lead to legal issues. It's crucial to understand the boundaries before you start scraping, especially when scraping large amounts of data.

Here are some key ethical and legal considerations:

- **Terms of Service (TOS):** Always check the website's TOS to see if scraping is permitted. Many websites prohibit scraping entirely, while others may allow it under certain conditions.
- **robots.txt:** Websites often use a file called *robots.txt* to specify which pages or resources on their site can be scraped and which cannot. While this file isn't legally binding, respecting it is considered best practice.
- **Overloading Servers:** Web scraping can put a strain on a website's server, especially if you're making frequent

15

requests in a short period of time. This can negatively affect the website's performance for regular users.

- **right and Data Ownership:** If you're scraping content that is protected by right, such as images or proprietary text, be mindful of how you use that data. Reposting it without permission could lead to intellectual property violations.

- **Data Privacy Laws:** In some regions (e.g., the European Union under GDPR), scraping personal or private data can violate privacy laws. Always ensure that the data you're scraping doesn't breach privacy regulations.

Being mindful of these issues not only helps you avoid legal trouble but also builds trust with the online community. Responsible scraping ensures that you're not only following the rules but also respecting the websites you're interacting with.

Why Python?

Python has become the go-to language for web scraping, and for good reason. Here's why Python stands out:

- **Simplicity and Readability:** Python's syntax is clean and easy to understand, making it an excellent choice for beginners. You don't need to deal with complicated or verbose code to accomplish tasks, and this simplicity allows you to focus on the task at hand: scraping and analyzing data.

- **Libraries for Web Scraping:** Python has a rich ecosystem of libraries specifically designed for web scraping. Libraries like BeautifulSoup, Requests, and Selenium make scraping straightforward and efficient, providing a wide range of functionality out of the box.

- **Community and Support:** Python has a massive, active community, meaning you can find help and resources for almost anything. Whether you're troubleshooting a specific problem or looking for a library to handle a specific task, the community is there to help.

- **Versatility:** Python is not only great for web scraping but also for processing and analyzing the data you scrape. With libraries like Pandas, NumPy, and Matplotlib, Python can handle everything from cleaning and structuring your data to performing statistical analysis and visualizing results.

Overview of Python Libraries for Web Scraping

Python offers several libraries that make web scraping easy and efficient. Below is an overview of the key libraries you'll use throughout this book:

- **Requests:** The Requests library is a simple HTTP library that allows you to send HTTP requests and retrieve data from a website. It's the easiest way to interact with web pages from your Python code. You'll use it to make GET and POST requests to retrieve the raw HTML of a page.

- **BeautifulSoup:** Once you have the HTML content of a page, BeautifulSoup is used to parse and navigate it. It creates a tree-like structure from the HTML, allowing you to easily find and extract data from the page. BeautifulSoup supports both searching and navigating the DOM (Document Object Model) tree, making it ideal for extracting specific elements like paragraphs, links, and tables.

- **Selenium:** While BeautifulSoup is great for static web pages, many modern websites load data dynamically using JavaScript. Selenium allows you to control a web browser programmatically, rendering JavaScript content and allowing you to scrape data from these dynamic pages. It's particularly useful when scraping pages that require user interaction or when you need to deal with complex page structures.

- **lxml:** lxml is a powerful and efficient XML and HTML parsing library. It can be used as an alternative to BeautifulSoup for parsing HTML, and it's known for its performance and speed, especially when handling large pages.

- **Pandas:** After scraping the data, you'll often want to analyze it. Pandas is the go-to library for working with structured data in Python. It allows you to store scraped data in a DataFrame, which makes it easy to manipulate, filter, and analyze.

- **Regex (re):** Regular expressions are used for advanced text searching and pattern matching. While BeautifulSoup is great for selecting elements by tag, class, or ID, Regex can be used to find more complex patterns in the scraped data, such as phone numbers, email addresses, or product codes.

Setting Up Your Python Environment

Before we dive into scraping, you need to set up your Python environment. Here's a quick guide on how to do that:

1. **Install   Python:**
   If you don't have Python installed, you can download the latest version from the official Python website: https://www.python.org/downloads/. Follow the instructions for your operating system (Windows, macOS, or Linux). Make sure to add Python to your system's PATH during the installation process.

2. **Install   pip   (Python   Package   Installer):**
   Pip is the default package manager for Python, and it

comes installed with Python 3.4 and later. If for some reason it's not installed, you can follow the instructions on the pip installation guide.

3. **Install Necessary Libraries:** To get started with web scraping, you need to install the libraries we'll be using. Open a terminal or command prompt and run the following commands:

```bash
Edit
pip install requests
pip install beautifulsoup4
pip install selenium
pip install pandas
pip install lxml
```

You may also need to install a web driver for Selenium (such as ChromeDriver or GeckoDriver) depending on the browser you intend to use.

Conclusion of Chapter 1

This chapter provided an introduction to the essentials of web scraping: what it is, why it matters, and why Python is the ideal language for the task. We also touched on the ethical and legal considerations, ensuring that your scraping practices are both effective and responsible. In the following chapters, we'll dive deeper into the tools and techniques that will allow you to scrape websites and extract valuable data in a structured and meaningful way.

CHAPTER 2

GETTING STARTED WITH BEAUTIFULSOUP

In this chapter, we'll dive into **BeautifulSoup**, one of the most powerful and user-friendly Python libraries for web scraping. BeautifulSoup helps you parse HTML and XML documents, allowing you to easily navigate and extract useful information from web pages. By the end of this chapter, you'll have a solid understanding of how BeautifulSoup works and be equipped with the basics for scraping and parsing web content.

Introduction to BeautifulSoup and Its Features

BeautifulSoup is a Python library designed for parsing HTML and XML documents and providing a structured interface for navigating the data. It creates a tree-like structure from the raw HTML, allowing you to easily access elements, attributes, and content.

Here's why **BeautifulSoup** is a go-to tool for web scraping:

- **Ease of Use:** BeautifulSoup simplifies the task of navigating and searching through an HTML document. Its

API is intuitive, and it's designed to handle imperfect HTML gracefully, making it robust even when dealing with poorly formatted web pages.

- **Search Capabilities:** BeautifulSoup allows you to search the HTML tree by tags, attributes, or text. You can select elements using a wide variety of methods, which makes it easy to extract the data you need.

- **Supports Multiple Parsers:** BeautifulSoup works with multiple parsers, including Python's built-in `html.parser` and other faster parsers like `lxml` or `html5lib`. This flexibility helps you choose the most efficient parser for your needs.

- **Compatibility:** BeautifulSoup works well with both static and dynamic content (when paired with libraries like Selenium). It allows you to easily extract data, even when websites have complex structures.

Installation and Setup

Before you can start using BeautifulSoup, you need to install it and set up your environment. Follow these steps to get everything ready for web scraping:

1. **Install BeautifulSoup and Requests:**

If you don't have BeautifulSoup installed, you can install it using pip. Along with BeautifulSoup, we'll also install the **Requests** library, which helps us fetch HTML content from a website.

In your terminal or command prompt, run the following:

```bash
Edit
pip install beautifulsoup4 requests
```

This command will install both libraries. Requests will help you download the raw HTML content of web pages, while BeautifulSoup will handle parsing and navigating that content.

2. **Verify Installation:**

After installation, verify that everything is set up correctly. Open a Python interactive shell or a script and run:

```python
Edit
import requests
from bs4 import BeautifulSoup

# Test fetching and parsing a page
```

24

```
url = 'https://example.com'  # Replace with
a real URL
response = requests.get(url)
soup   =   BeautifulSoup(response.content,
'html.parser')

print(soup.prettify())    #  Display  the
prettified HTML of the page
```

This code fetches the content from a website (replace `https://example.com` with a URL of your choice), parses it with BeautifulSoup, and then prints the HTML structure in a readable, indented format.

Understanding HTML and Parsing with BeautifulSoup

To effectively use BeautifulSoup, it's important to understand how HTML is structured. HTML documents are made up of elements that define the structure and content of a web page. Each element has:

- **Tags:** These are the basic building blocks of HTML and define the start and end of an element, e.g., `<p></p>` for a paragraph or `<a></a>` for a link.
- **Attributes:** Tags can have attributes, which provide additional information about the element. For example, an `<a>` tag may have an `href` attribute that points to a link

destination   (`<a`
`href="https://example.com">Click here</a>`).

- **Text Content:** Most tags contain text or other elements
  inside them, such as `<h1>Header</h1>` or `<p>This is`
  `a paragraph.</p>`.

BeautifulSoup allows you to parse and interact with these
components in a Pythonic way. It creates a **BeautifulSoup object**
that acts like a parsed HTML tree. You can then navigate the tree
to find tags, attributes, and text content.

Example:

Consider the following HTML:

```
html
Edit
<html>
  <body>
    <h1>Welcome to My Website</h1>
    <p>This is a paragraph.</p>
    <a href="https://example.com">Click here</a>
  </body>
</html>
```

If you parse this HTML with BeautifulSoup, you can access each
element like so:

```
python
```

```
Edit
html = """
<html>
  <body>
    <h1>Welcome to My Website</h1>
    <p>This is a paragraph.</p>
    <a href="https://example.com">Click here</a>
  </body>
</html>
"""


soup = BeautifulSoup(html, 'html.parser')


# Accessing tags
print(soup.h1)   # <h1>Welcome to My Website</h1>
print(soup.p)    # <p>This is a paragraph.</p>
print(soup.a)                              #        <a
href="https://example.com">Click here</a>


# Accessing attributes
print(soup.a['href'])   # https://example.com
```

Basic Parsing Techniques (Tags, Attributes, and Text)

Now that we have a basic understanding of HTML, let's look at some of the core techniques you'll use to parse HTML with BeautifulSoup:

1. **Selecting Tags:**

To select an HTML tag, you can simply access it by its tag name. For example:

```python
Edit
# Select the first <h1> tag
h1_tag = soup.h1
print(h1_tag)        #   <h1>Welcome   to   My
Website</h1>
```

You can also use the `find_all()` method to select all occurrences of a tag:

```python
Edit
# Find all <p> tags
paragraphs = soup.find_all('p')
for p in paragraphs:
    print(p)
```

2. **Accessing Tag Attributes:**

HTML tags can have attributes, such as `href` in an anchor tag (`<a>`). You can access these attributes directly:

```python
Edit
```

```
# Accessing the 'href' attribute of the <a>
tag
link = soup.a
print(link['href'])   # https://example.com
```

3. **Extracting Text Content:**

To get the text content of an element (i.e., the inner HTML), use the .text property:

```python
Edit
# Extracting text from the <h1> tag
h1_text = soup.h1.text
print(h1_text)   # Welcome to My Website
```

4. **Using CSS Selectors:**

BeautifulSoup also supports CSS selectors, which allow you to select tags based on classes, IDs, and other attributes. You can use the select() method:

```python
Edit
# Select a tag by its CSS class
p_tag = soup.select('p')
print(p_tag)        #   [<p>This   is   a
paragraph.</p>]
```

Conclusion of Chapter 2

In this chapter, we've explored the core concepts of using **BeautifulSoup** to scrape and parse web pages. You've learned about the basic structure of HTML documents, how to install and set up BeautifulSoup, and how to use it to navigate through HTML tags, access attributes, and extract text content. These fundamental skills will serve as the foundation for more advanced techniques in future chapters, where you'll learn how to scrape dynamic content, handle complex data, and perform more intricate tasks.

With these tools at your disposal, you're ready to start scraping websites and extracting meaningful data!

CHAPTER 3

THE ANATOMY OF A WEB PAGE

In this chapter, we'll break down the components of a web page to help you understand how data is structured. Knowing how HTML is organized and how you can navigate its structure is critical for successful web scraping. By understanding the anatomy of a web page, you'll be better equipped to identify the data you want to scrape and select it efficiently using BeautifulSoup.

Understanding HTML Structure

HTML (HyperText Markup Language) is the standard language used to create and structure content on the web. An HTML document is essentially a tree of elements that define the structure of a webpage. Each webpage has a **root element** (usually the <html> tag), which contains other nested elements like <head>, <body>, and various content tags such as <p>, <div>, and <a>.

Here's a simple example of an HTML structure:

```
html
Edit
<!DOCTYPE html>
<html>
```

31

```
<head>
  <title>Sample Web Page</title>
</head>
<body>
  <h1>Welcome to My Web Page</h1>
  <p>This is a paragraph.</p>
  <a href="https://example.com">Click here</a>
</body>
</html>
```

In this structure:

- The `<html>` tag is the root of the document.
- The `<head>` section contains metadata like the title of the page.
- The `<body>` section contains the visible content on the page.
- Inside the `<body>`, we have various tags like `<h1>` for headings, `<p>` for paragraphs, and `<a>` for links.

Key Components: HTML Tags, Elements, and Attributes

To effectively scrape data, it's essential to understand the following key components of an HTML document:

1. **HTML Tags:**

Tags are the building blocks of HTML. They define the structure and type of content in the document. Tags are usually written in pairs: an opening tag and a closing tag. For example:

```
html
Edit
<p>This is a paragraph.</p>
```

In this example, <p> is the opening tag, and </p> is the closing tag. Everything in between is the content of the tag.

2. **HTML Elements:**

An **element** refers to an entire set of HTML tags and their content. For example:

```
html
Edit
<a         href="https://example.com">Click
here</a>
```

The <a> tag and its content ("Click here") form the entire **anchor element**, including the attribute (href="https://example.com") that specifies the link destination.

3. **Attributes:**

Tags can also have **attributes**, which provide additional information about the element. Attributes usually appear in the opening tag. For instance:

```
html
Edit
<a            href="https://example.com"
target="_blank">Visit our site</a>
```

In this case, `href` and `target` are attributes of the `<a>` tag, and their values are `"https://example.com"` and `"_blank"`, respectively. Attributes allow you to define specific properties, such as links, images, classes, and IDs.

Navigating a Page's Source Code

When you open a webpage in a browser, the page appears visually, but underneath, the browser interprets the page's **source code**. This source code is written in HTML (with optional CSS for styling and JavaScript for dynamic functionality).

To access the source code of a page, you can:

1. **Right-click** on the webpage and select **View Page Source** (in most browsers).

2. Alternatively, use the **Inspect Element** tool (usually accessed by right-clicking and selecting **Inspect**). This tool opens a panel where you can see the live HTML structure, CSS styles, and even JavaScript elements that power the page.

The page source is often overwhelming, but it's the key to scraping. You'll need to locate the part of the page that contains the data you want to extract.

Real-World Example: Inspecting a Page's Structure

Let's go through a real-world example of how you would inspect and understand the structure of a web page for scraping.

1. **Example Web Page:** Imagine you want to scrape a webpage listing books, and you're interested in getting the book titles and their prices.
2. **View Page Source:**
   - Open the webpage in a browser.
   - Right-click on the page and select **Inspect** (or use **View Page Source**).
   - You'll see the HTML code that renders the page.
3. **Identify Key Elements:** In the page source, search for the data you're interested in. For example, the books might

be listed as `<div>` elements with specific class names. Here's a sample section of HTML:

```
html
Edit
<div class="book-item">
  <h2     class="book-title">The      Great
Gatsby</h2>
  <p class="price">$10.99</p>
</div>
<div class="book-item">
  <h2     class="book-title">To     Kill     a
Mockingbird</h2>
  <p class="price">$12.50</p>
</div>
```

In this example:

- o Each book is contained in a `<div class="book-item">`.
- o The book title is inside an `<h2 class="book-title">`.
- o The price is in a `<p class="price">`.

4. **Inspecting Attributes:** Attributes often help identify elements more specifically. For instance, if the `<div>` tags have different classes for each book, you can use these classes to select the right elements.

- o Book title: You can select all titles with the `class="book-title"`.
- o Price: You can select all prices with the `class="price"`.

Using this information, you can create a scraping script to extract the book titles and prices from the page.

How to Navigate HTML in BeautifulSoup

Once you understand the structure of a page, you can use **BeautifulSoup** to extract the data. Here's how you might approach scraping the book titles and prices from the example above:

```python
python
Edit
import requests
from bs4 import BeautifulSoup

# Fetch the webpage content
url = 'https://example.com/books'
response = requests.get(url)

# Parse the HTML with BeautifulSoup
soup       =        BeautifulSoup(response.content,
'html.parser')
```

```
# Extract book titles and prices
books = soup.find_all('div', class_='book-item')

for book in books:
    title  =   book.find('h2,   class_='book-
title').text
    price = book.find('p', class_='price').text
    print(f'Title: {title}, Price: {price}')
```

In this code:

- `find_all()` is used to retrieve all <div> elements with the class `book-item`.
- `find()` is then used within each `book` element to extract the book title and price.

Conclusion of Chapter 3

Understanding the anatomy of a web page is crucial to effective web scraping. In this chapter, we've explored how HTML is structured, the roles of tags, elements, and attributes, and how you can navigate a page's source code to locate the data you want to scrape. You've also learned how to apply this knowledge in real-world scenarios by inspecting a page's structure and selecting relevant elements.

With this knowledge, you're now equipped to identify the components you need for scraping in future chapters, and you can start building more complex scraping strategies.

CHAPTER 4

SELECTING ELEMENTS WITH CSS SELECTORS

In this chapter, we'll dive into **CSS selectors**, a powerful and flexible way to identify and select elements on a web page. CSS selectors are commonly used in web development to style elements, but they are also invaluable for web scraping. By the end of this chapter, you'll be able to harness the full power of CSS selectors in BeautifulSoup to scrape data more efficiently.

Understanding CSS Selectors

CSS (Cascading Style Sheets) selectors are patterns used to select and manipulate HTML elements based on their attributes, such as IDs, classes, types, and relationships to other elements. They're widely used for styling web pages, but their flexibility also makes them perfect for scraping data.

Here are some common CSS selectors:

1. **Element Selector:** Targets an element by its tag name.
   - Example: p targets all <p> tags.

40

2. **Class Selector:** Targets elements with a specific class attribute.

   o Example: `.price` selects all elements with the class `price`.

3. **ID Selector:** Targets an element with a specific ID attribute.

   o Example: `#header` selects the element with the ID `header`.

4. **Descendant Selector:** Selects elements that are nested within a specified parent element.

   o Example: `div p` selects all `<p>` tags inside a `<div>` tag.

5. **Attribute Selector:** Selects elements based on the presence or value of an attribute.

   o Example: `a[href]` selects all `<a>` tags with an `href` attribute.

6. **Universal Selector:** Targets all elements on the page.

   o Example: `*` selects all elements.

Here's an example of using these selectors in a real-world HTML snippet:

```html
Edit
<div class="product">
  <h2 class="product-title">Laptop</h2>
  <p class="price">$999</p>
```

```
<a         href="https://example.com/laptop">Buy
now</a>
</div>
```

In this example:

- `.product-title` targets the product title.
- `.price` targets the price.
- `a[href]` can select the link that leads to the product page.

Using BeautifulSoup's select() Method

The `select()` method in BeautifulSoup allows you to select elements using **CSS selectors**. This method is incredibly versatile and supports all the common CSS selectors we've mentioned, including classes, IDs, and attributes.

The `select()` method returns a list of elements that match the given selector. Here's how to use it:

```python
Edit
from bs4 import BeautifulSoup

html = """
<div class="product">
  <h2 class="product-title">Laptop</h2>
  <p class="price">$999</p>
```

```
    <a        href="https://example.com/laptop">Buy
now</a>
</div>
"""

soup = BeautifulSoup(html, 'html.parser')

# Select elements using CSS selectors
title = soup.select('.product-title')
price = soup.select('.price')
link = soup.select('a[href]')

# Print the results
print(title[0].text)   # Laptop
print(price[0].text)   # $999
print(link[0]['href'])                        #
https://example.com/laptop
```

In this example:

- We use `.product-title` to select the product title.
- We use `.price` to select the price.
- We use `a[href]` to select the link with an `href` attribute.

The `select()` method is a more powerful and flexible way of navigating HTML compared to methods like `find()` and `find_all()`, especially when dealing with more complex selectors or nested elements.

Practical Example: Scraping with CSS Selectors

Let's apply what we've learned in a practical example. Imagine you're scraping a website that lists products, and you want to extract the product names, prices, and links.

Here's the HTML of the page:

```html
Edit
<div class="product-list">
  <div class="product">
    <h2 class="product-title">Laptop</h2>
    <p class="price">$999</p>
    <a    href="https://example.com/laptop">View
Product</a>
  </div>
  <div class="product">
    <h2 class="product-title">Smartphone</h2>
    <p class="price">$699</p>
    <a
href="https://example.com/smartphone">View
Product</a>
  </div>
</div>
```

Now, let's write a Python script using BeautifulSoup to scrape the product names, prices, and links:

```python
Edit
import requests
from bs4 import BeautifulSoup

# Sample URL (replace with a real URL)
url = 'https://example.com/products'

# Fetch the page content
response = requests.get(url)
soup      =       BeautifulSoup(response.content,
'html.parser')

# Select all product elements
products = soup.select('.product')

# Loop through each product and extract the
relevant data
for product in products:
    title      =       product.select('.product-
title')[0].text
    price = product.select('.price')[0].text
    link = product.select('a[href]')[0]['href']

    print(f'Product: {title}, Price: {price},
Link: {link}')
```

This script:

1. Fetches the content from a webpage (replace `url` with the actual URL).
2. Selects all the products by targeting `.product`.
3. Loops through each product and extracts the product title, price, and link.
4. Prints the scraped data for each product.

Best Practices for Selecting Elements

When working with CSS selectors, it's essential to follow best practices to make your code efficient and resilient to changes in the web page structure.

1. **Be Specific:** The more specific your CSS selector, the less likely it is to break if the website structure changes. Instead of using broad selectors like `div`, target elements by their classes or IDs (e.g., `.product-title` or `#product-list`).

2. **Use Classes and IDs:** Classes (`.class`) and IDs (`#id`) are often the most reliable way to target elements because they are unique or commonly used for specific purposes. They also make your code easier to read and maintain.

3. **Avoid Overly Complex Selectors:** While you can chain multiple CSS selectors together (e.g., `div.product > h2.product-title`), it's better to avoid overly complex selectors that are difficult to read or maintain.

4. **Use Attribute Selectors When Needed:** If elements don't have unique classes or IDs, use attribute selectors. For example, you can select all links (`<a>`) with an `href` attribute using `a[href]`.

5. **Handle Missing Elements Gracefully:** When using the `select()` method, be aware that it may return an empty list if the selector doesn't match any elements. Always check if the list is non-empty before attempting to access the elements:

```python
Edit
title = soup.select('.product-title')
if title:
    print(title[0].text)
else:
    print('Title not found')
```

Conclusion of Chapter 4

In this chapter, we've explored how to use **CSS selectors** in **BeautifulSoup** to select and scrape elements from web pages. You've learned the basics of CSS selectors, how to use the `select()` method in BeautifulSoup, and how to scrape data with real-world examples. By following best practices for selecting elements, you can ensure your scraping scripts are efficient, readable, and less prone to breaking when the website structure changes.

With this powerful technique in your toolkit, you're ready to scrape more complex web pages in future chapters.

CHAPTER 5

NAVIGATING THE PARSE TREE

In this chapter, we'll delve into how to navigate the **parse tree** of an HTML document. When BeautifulSoup parses an HTML document, it transforms it into a tree structure, where each tag in the document is a node. Understanding this tree and how to navigate it is crucial for selecting and extracting the data you need. We'll cover BeautifulSoup's navigation methods, demonstrate how to traverse complex structures, and address how to handle nested elements and tables.

Tree Structure of HTML Documents

An HTML document can be visualized as a tree structure, where the elements are nodes in the tree. The top-most node is the **root element** (typically the <html> tag), and from there, the document branches out into other tags like <head>, <body>, <div>, <p>, and so on.

Consider this simple HTML structure:

```
html
Edit
<html>
```

49

```
<head>
  <title>My Page</title>
</head>
<body>
  <h1>Welcome to My Web Page</h1>
  <div class="content">
    <p>This is a paragraph.</p>
    <a         href="https://example.com">Click
here</a>
  </div>
</body>
</html>
```

The parse tree for this document would look something like this:

```php-template
Edit
<html>
 ├── <head>
 │     └── <title>My Page</title>
 └── <body>
       ├── <h1>Welcome to My Web Page</h1>
       └── <div class="content">
             ├── <p>This is a paragraph.</p>
             └──                              <a
href="https://example.com">Click here</a>
```

Each tag is a node, and the relationships between the tags form a parent-child structure, with **siblings** representing tags that share the same parent.

Using BeautifulSoup's Navigation Methods

BeautifulSoup provides several methods to navigate through the parse tree, enabling you to access parent, child, and sibling elements. Here are some key methods for navigating the tree:

1. **Navigating to Parent Elements:**

   The parent attribute allows you to access the immediate parent of a tag. If you're inside a tag and want to trace back to its parent, this is your method.

   ```python
   Edit
   soup    =    BeautifulSoup('<div><p>Hello
   World!</p></div>', 'html.parser')
   p_tag = soup.find('p')
   parent_tag = p_tag.parent
   print(parent_tag)        #    <div><p>Hello
   World!</p></div>
   ```

   In this case, the <p> tag's parent is the <div> tag.

2. **Navigating to Child Elements:**

   To get the immediate children of an element, you can use the children attribute. This returns an iterator, which you can loop through to access each child tag.

51

```python
Edit
soup                                        =
BeautifulSoup('<div><p>Hello</p><p>World!
</p></div>', 'html.parser')
div_tag = soup.find('div')
for child in div_tag.children:
    print(child)
```

This will print each child of the `<div>` tag, which includes the two `<p>` tags.

3. **Navigating to Sibling Elements:**

To access the siblings of an element, you can use the `next_sibling` and `previous_sibling` attributes.

- o   `next_sibling`: Moves to the next element on the same level.
- o   `previous_sibling`: Moves to the previous element.

```python
Edit
soup                                        =
BeautifulSoup('<div><p>First</p><p>Second
</p></div>', 'html.parser')
first_p = soup.find('p')
second_p = first_p.find_next_sibling('p')
```

```
print(second_p)  # <p>Second</p>
```

Here, we access the second <p> tag by moving to the next sibling of the first <p>.

4. **Accessing All Descendants:**

To access all descendants (children, grandchildren, etc.), you can use the descendants attribute. This returns an iterator that lets you loop through all tags within an element.

```python
Edit
soup = BeautifulSoup('<div><p>Hello</p><a
href="#">Link</a></div>', 'html.parser')
div_tag = soup.find('div')
for descendant in div_tag.descendants:
    print(descendant)
```

This will print the <p> and <a> tags as well as their text content.

Practical Examples of Navigating Complex Structures

HTML pages often contain deeply nested elements or complex structures. Let's take a look at a more complex example to see how you can navigate and extract data from such structures.

53

Imagine you are scraping a blog page that has the following structure:

```html
Edit
<div class="post">
  <h1 class="title">Blog Post 1</h1>
  <div class="content">
    <p>First paragraph.</p>
    <p>Second paragraph.</p>
    <a href="https://example.com/read-more">Read
more</a>
  </div>
</div>
<div class="post">
  <h1 class="title">Blog Post 2</h1>
  <div class="content">
    <p>Third paragraph.</p>
    <p>Fourth paragraph.</p>
    <a href="https://example.com/read-more">Read
more</a>
  </div>
</div>
```

To scrape the titles of all posts, you would:

```python
Edit
from bs4 import BeautifulSoup
```

```python
html = """
<div class="post">
  <h1 class="title">Blog Post 1</h1>
  <div class="content">
    <p>First paragraph.</p>
    <p>Second paragraph.</p>
    <a href="https://example.com/read-more">Read
more</a>
  </div>
</div>
<div class="post">
  <h1 class="title">Blog Post 2</h1>
  <div class="content">
    <p>Third paragraph.</p>
    <p>Fourth paragraph.</p>
    <a href="https://example.com/read-more">Read
more</a>
  </div>
</div>
"""


soup = BeautifulSoup(html, 'html.parser')

# Find all posts
posts = soup.find_all('div', class_='post')

# Loop through each post and print its title
for post in posts:
    title = post.find('h1', class_='title').text
```

55

```
    print(title)
```

This script will output:

```
nginx
Edit
Blog Post 1
Blog Post 2
```

Here, we've used the `find_all()` method to grab all `<div>` elements with the class `post`. Then, for each post, we extract the title from the `<h1>` tag.

Handling Nested Elements and Tables

Web scraping often involves extracting data from **nested elements** or **tables**. Let's see how BeautifulSoup helps you navigate through them:

Handling Nested Elements:

When elements are nested inside one another, you can chain your navigation methods to get to the desired tag. For example:

```
html
Edit
<div class="post">
  <h1 class="title">Nested Example</h1>
```

```
<div class="content">
  <p>This  is  inside  a  nested  <span>span
element</span>.</p>
  </div>
</div>
```

To extract the `<span>` text inside the nested paragraph, you can do:

```python
Edit
soup  =  BeautifulSoup('<div  class="post"><h1
class="title">Nested           Example</h1><div
class="content"><p>This  is  inside  a  nested
<span>span     element</span>.</p></div></div>',
'html.parser')

span_text = soup.find('span').text
print(span_text)  # span element
```
Handling Tables:

HTML tables can be tricky because they often have complex row and column structures. Here's an example:

```html
Edit
<table>
  <tr>
    <th>Title</th>
```

```
  <th>Author</th>
 </tr>
 <tr>
   <td>The Great Gatsby</td>
   <td>F. Scott Fitzgerald</td>
 </tr>
 <tr>
   <td>1984</td>
   <td>George Orwell</td>
 </tr>
</table>
```

To extract the titles and authors from the table:

```python
Edit
soup = BeautifulSoup('''
<table>
  <tr><th>Title</th><th>Author</th></tr>
  <tr><td>The   Great   Gatsby</td><td>F.   Scott
Fitzgerald</td></tr>
  <tr><td>1984</td><td>George Orwell</td></tr>
</table>
''', 'html.parser')

# Find all rows in the table
rows = soup.find_all('tr')[1:]  # Skip header row

for row in rows:
    cols = row.find_all('td')
```

```
title = cols[0].text
author = cols[1].text
print(f"Title: {title}, Author: {author}")
```

This script will output:

```
yaml
Edit
Title:   The   Great   Gatsby,   Author:   F.   Scott
Fitzgerald
Title: 1984, Author: George Orwell
```

Conclusion of Chapter 5

Navigating the parse tree of an HTML document is an essential skill for web scraping. In this chapter, you learned how HTML documents are structured as trees, and how to use BeautifulSoup's navigation methods—like `parent`, `children`, and `siblings`—to traverse these trees. You also saw practical examples of how to handle complex structures, nested elements, and tables.

With these skills, you can now move forward with more advanced scraping tasks, and tackle even more complicated web pages with ease.

CHAPTER 6

SCRAPING DYNAMIC CONTENT

In this chapter, we will explore the challenges associated with scraping dynamic web pages—those that rely on **AJAX** and **JavaScript** to load content asynchronously. Static pages, which are served directly from the server as HTML, are easier to scrape since the content is readily available in the source code. However, many modern websites use JavaScript to dynamically load content after the initial page load, which makes scraping them a bit more complicated. We will discuss the key concepts behind dynamic content, the challenges you might face, and how to overcome them using **Selenium** combined with **BeautifulSoup**.

Understanding Dynamic Content (AJAX, JavaScript)

Dynamic content refers to data that is not loaded directly in the initial HTML page. Instead, it is loaded through **JavaScript** after the page has loaded, often via asynchronous requests using **AJAX (Asynchronous JavaScript and XML)**. This allows websites to update or modify content dynamically without needing to reload the entire page. Examples of dynamic content include live sports scores, stock market updates, product prices, and social media feeds.

AJAX in Web Scraping

AJAX enables the webpage to make background requests to the server and receive data without refreshing the page. This data is typically rendered and injected into the HTML structure dynamically by JavaScript. To understand how to scrape dynamic content, we need to know how it is being injected into the page.

For example, when you visit a page, you might see a list of blog posts that load only after the page has finished loading. The HTML source code you initially view doesn't contain the blog post content directly. Instead, JavaScript requests the data from the server and populates it into the DOM.

Challenges with Scraping JavaScript-loaded Content

When scraping dynamic content, there are a few key challenges:

1. **Content Not in Initial HTML Source:** Since JavaScript modifies the DOM after the page loads, traditional scraping methods (like using BeautifulSoup alone) will not capture the dynamically loaded content. BeautifulSoup only parses the static HTML content that is available at the time the page is initially served.

2. **AJAX Requests:** Some content is loaded via AJAX calls, and these requests may return data in JSON or XML

61

format rather than HTML. To scrape this kind of content, you need to inspect the network requests to identify the API endpoints that return the data.

3. **JavaScript Rendering:** In some cases, entire elements, including complex visual components (like maps, charts, or data tables), are rendered by JavaScript. If the data is hidden behind JavaScript execution, it won't appear in the static HTML.

Solutions: Using Selenium with BeautifulSoup

To scrape dynamic content, you can use **Selenium**, a browser automation tool that can render JavaScript just like a real browser. Selenium simulates a real user interaction with a website and allows you to extract the dynamically loaded content. Once the page is fully rendered, you can pass the HTML to BeautifulSoup for parsing and data extraction.

Using Selenium with BeautifulSoup

1. **Install Selenium:** To use Selenium, you need to install it and also have a driver for a web browser (e.g., ChromeDriver for Google Chrome). You can install Selenium with `pip`:

```bash
Edit
```

```
pip install selenium
```

You also need to download the appropriate **driver** for the browser you're using. For Chrome, you can download **ChromeDriver** from the official site.

2. **Setup and Initialize Selenium:** Below is a basic example of how to use Selenium to navigate a page and extract content after it has been rendered by JavaScript.

```python
Edit
from selenium import webdriver
from bs4 import BeautifulSoup

# Path to your ChromeDriver
driver_path = 'path_to_chromedriver'

# Start the Selenium WebDriver
driver = webdriver.Chrome(driver_path)

# Open a dynamic page
driver.get('https://example.com')

# Wait for content to load (optional)
driver.implicitly_wait(5)   # Wait up to 5
seconds

# Get the rendered HTML
```

63

```
html = driver.page_source

# Parse the HTML with BeautifulSoup
soup = BeautifulSoup(html, 'html.parser')

# Now you can use BeautifulSoup to find the
content you need
content            =            soup.find('div',
class_='content')
print(content.text)

# Close the browser
driver.quit()
```

In this example:

- o We initialize Selenium to launch Chrome and navigate to the dynamic page.
- o We wait for the content to load (`implicitly_wait`).
- o After the page has loaded, we use Selenium to get the page's source (`page_source`), which includes both the static and dynamic content.
- o Finally, we pass the HTML to BeautifulSoup to extract the desired information.

3. **Handling Dynamic Page Elements:** You can use **Selenium's explicit waits** to wait for specific elements to be loaded before continuing the scraping process. This

ensures that you scrape data only after all necessary JavaScript and AJAX requests have been completed.

```python
Edit
from selenium.webdriver.common.by import By
from selenium.webdriver.support.ui import WebDriverWait
from selenium.webdriver.support import expected_conditions as EC

# Wait until a specific element is loaded
element = WebDriverWait(driver, 10).until(

EC.presence_of_element_located((By.ID,
'target-element-id'))
)
```

4. **Extracting Data from AJAX Requests:** If a website loads content via AJAX, you can inspect the network traffic using your browser's Developer Tools to identify the API requests responsible for retrieving the data. Once you have the API endpoint, you can make a direct HTTP request to that endpoint using a library like `requests` and parse the response.

Here's an example using `requests` to fetch data from an API directly:

```python
Edit
import requests

url = 'https://example.com/api/data'
response = requests.get(url)
data = response.json()  # Assuming the data
is returned as JSON
print(data)
```

This approach bypasses the need for Selenium by directly accessing the API used by the website.

Real-world Example: Scraping a Dynamic Page

Let's look at an example of scraping a page that loads content dynamically. Suppose you want to scrape product prices from a webpage that loads product listings via AJAX:

1. **Inspect the Page:** Open the page in your browser and use the Developer Tools (F12) to inspect the network activity. Look for an AJAX request (usually with a `GET` method) that returns product data in a format like JSON.

2. **Extracting the Product Data:** Use Selenium to load the page and inspect the content:

```python
Edit
```

```python
from selenium import webdriver
from bs4 import BeautifulSoup

driver = webdriver.Chrome(driver_path)
driver.get('https://example.com/products'
)

# Wait for the product list to load
driver.implicitly_wait(5)

# Get the rendered HTML
html = driver.page_source
soup = BeautifulSoup(html, 'html.parser')

# Extract product names and prices
products       =       soup.find_all('div',
class_='product')
for product in products:
    name = product.find('h2').text
    price      =       product.find('span',
class_='price').text
    print(f'Product:    {name},    Price:
{price}')

driver.quit()
```

In this case, Selenium waits for the dynamic content to load, and BeautifulSoup is used to extract the product names and prices.

Conclusion of Chapter 6

Scraping dynamic content introduces several challenges, particularly when JavaScript and AJAX are involved. In this chapter, you've learned about the limitations of scraping JavaScript-loaded content with BeautifulSoup alone and how to use Selenium to work around these limitations. We also covered how to access AJAX-based data by inspecting network traffic and making direct API requests. By combining Selenium's dynamic content rendering capabilities with BeautifulSoup's parsing power, you can scrape complex websites with ease, even when the content is loaded asynchronously.

As you continue, this knowledge will enable you to handle more advanced scraping scenarios and extract data from websites that rely on dynamic loading techniques.

CHAPTER 7

HANDLING DIFFERENT DATA TYPES

In this chapter, we will explore how to handle various data types while scraping web pages. Web pages contain a variety of data formats, including **text, numbers, links, images, multimedia,** and **forms**. Understanding how to extract and process these different data types efficiently is a crucial skill for any web scraper. We will walk through techniques to extract and manage each of these data types, and provide real-world examples to illustrate their practical use.

Extracting Text, Numbers, and Links

Web scraping often begins with extracting basic textual data from HTML elements. BeautifulSoup allows you to access this data easily by navigating the structure of the HTML and finding specific tags, classes, or IDs. Below are some common tasks:

1. **Extracting Text:** Most web pages contain textual information that you might want to scrape, such as titles, headings, or paragraphs. BeautifulSoup's `text` attribute allows you to extract this easily from HTML tags.

```python
Edit
from bs4 import BeautifulSoup

html = """
<html>
  <head><title>Example Page</title></head>
  <body>
    <h1>Welcome to the Example Page</h1>
    <p>This is an example of scraping
text.</p>
  </body>
</html>
"""

soup = BeautifulSoup(html, 'html.parser')
title = soup.title.text
heading = soup.h1.text
paragraph = soup.p.text

print(title)   # Output: Example Page
print(heading)   # Output: Welcome to the
Example Page
print(paragraph)   # Output: This is an
example of scraping text.
```

In this example, we extract the text content from the
`<title>`, `<h1>`, and `<p>` tags.

2. **Extracting Numbers:** Numbers on a webpage can include prices, statistics, or any other data points. You may need to parse numbers and convert them into a numerical format for further analysis.

```python
Edit
price              =              soup.find('span',
class_='price').text
price       =       float(price.replace('$',
'').replace(',', ''))   # Clean and convert
to float
print(price)
```

This example shows how to extract a price (e.g., "$1,000") and convert it into a `float` for mathematical operations.

3. **Extracting Links:** Links are crucial for navigation and data gathering from other pages. To extract URLs from a webpage, you can use the `href` attribute of `<a>` tags.

```python
Edit
links = soup.find_all('a')
for link in links:
    href = link.get('href')
    print(href)
```

This will print all the URLs (`href` attributes) from the page. You can filter and process these links as needed (e.g., scraping data from linked pages).

Handling Images and Multimedia

Images and multimedia files are common elements in web scraping. These can be images, videos, or audio files that require special handling, particularly when downloading or saving them locally. Here's how you can handle different multimedia types.

1. **Extracting Image URLs:** To scrape images, you will need to extract the URLs from the `src` attribute of `<img>` tags. Once you have the URLs, you can download the images using `requests`.

   ```python
   Edit
   img_tags = soup.find_all('img')
   for img in img_tags:
       img_url = img.get('src')
       print(img_url)
   ```

   This code extracts the `src` attributes of all `<img>` tags. You can then use these URLs to download the images:

   ```python
   ```

```
Edit
import requests

img_url = 'https://example.com/image.jpg'
img_data = requests.get(img_url).content
with open('image.jpg', 'wb') as file:
    file.write(img_data)
```

2. **Handling Multimedia (Videos and Audio):** Videos and audio files are often embedded using tags like `<video>`, `<audio>`, or `<iframe>`. To extract the URL for multimedia files, you can access the `src` or `source` elements.

For videos:

```python
Edit
video_tags = soup.find_all('video')
for video in video_tags:
    video_url                      =
video.find('source').get('src')
    print(video_url)
```

For audio:

```python
Edit
audio_tags = soup.find_all('audio')
```

73

```
for audio in audio_tags:
    audio_url                              =
audio.find('source').get('src')
    print(audio_url)
```

These examples allow you to identify and extract video and audio file URLs from the HTML structure.

Working with Forms and Input Fields

Web forms are a significant part of many websites, and often, they are used to collect user input (e.g., search queries, signups, logins). Scraping data from forms requires identifying the `<form>` element and its associated input fields, buttons, and action attributes.

1. **Extracting Form Data:** The `form` tag in HTML represents a web form. Inside it, there are `<input>`, `<select>`, `<textarea>`, and `<button>` tags, all of which can be used to capture user input. Here's an example of how to extract information from a form.

```python
Edit
form = soup.find('form')
inputs = form.find_all('input')
for input_field in inputs:
```

```
print(input_field.get('name'),
input_field.get('value'))
```

This code extracts all input field names and values from a form. For forms that include dropdowns (`<select>` tags), checkboxes, or radio buttons, you would handle them similarly by extracting the values they contain.

2. **Handling Form Submission:** Sometimes, forms submit data to a server for processing. You might want to scrape data by automating form submissions. This can be done with the help of **Selenium** or **requests**. Using **Selenium**, you can simulate a user entering text and submitting the form.

```python
Edit
from selenium import webdriver
from selenium.webdriver.common.by import By

# Initialize WebDriver
driver = webdriver.Chrome()

# Navigate to the page with the form
driver.get('https://example.com/search')

# Find the input field and submit a search
term
```

```
search_box = driver.find_element(By.NAME,
'q')
search_box.send_keys('web scraping')
search_box.submit()

# Wait for results and extract data
driver.implicitly_wait(5)
results = driver.page_source
```

This example simulates typing into a search box and submitting the form, then retrieves the search results for further scraping.

Real-world Example: Scraping and Processing Different Data Types

Let's now put all of this together with a real-world example. Suppose you are scraping a product listing page from an e-commerce website. The page contains product names, prices, images, and links to individual product detail pages.

```python
Edit
import requests
from bs4 import BeautifulSoup

url = 'https://example.com/products'
response = requests.get(url)
```

```
soup         =         BeautifulSoup(response.text,
'html.parser')

# Extracting product names
product_names       =         soup.find_all('h2',
class_='product-name')
for name in product_names:
    print(f'Product: {name.text}')

# Extracting prices and converting to float
prices = soup.find_all('span', class_='price')
for price in prices:
    price_value = float(price.text.replace('$',
'').replace(',', ''))
    print(f'Price: ${price_value}')

# Extracting product image URLs
img_tags = soup.find_all('img', class_='product-
image')
for img in img_tags:
    img_url = img.get('src')
    print(f'Image URL: {img_url}')

# Extracting product detail page links
links    =    soup.find_all('a',    class_='product-
link')
for link in links:
    product_url = link.get('href')
    print(f'Product Link: {product_url}')
```

In this example, we are scraping various types of data:

- Product names from `<h2>` tags.
- Prices from `<span>` tags, converting the text to a numerical format.
- Image URLs from `<img>` tags.
- Links to product detail pages from `<a>` tags.

Conclusion of Chapter 7

Handling different data types is an essential skill for web scraping. Whether you are extracting text, numbers, multimedia content, or interacting with forms, the tools provided by BeautifulSoup allow you to efficiently gather the necessary data. Understanding how to navigate and process these data types ensures that you can scrape even the most complex websites effectively. This chapter gave you practical examples of how to extract and handle text, links, images, multimedia, and form data, which are fundamental to any web scraping project.

CHAPTER 8

SCRAPING MULTIPLE PAGES

In this chapter, we will explore how to scrape data from multiple pages, a common scenario in web scraping. Many websites divide content into multiple pages, especially when the data is extensive, such as product listings, search results, or articles. Handling pagination properly is essential to collect data across multiple pages. We'll discuss how to identify pagination elements, use loops to scrape data from several pages, and work with URL patterns in pagination. By the end of this chapter, you'll be able to automate the process of scraping across multiple pages efficiently.

Working with Pagination

Pagination is a technique used on websites to divide large amounts of content into separate pages. It is most often seen in search results, product listings, blog archives, etc. When scraping such pages, you need to handle the navigation through these multiple pages and collect the data from each one.

To start, let's explore how pagination works in a typical webpage.

1. **Identifying Pagination Elements:** Pagination elements are typically found at the bottom of a webpage, often in

the form of "Next", "Previous", or numbered links. To scrape multiple pages, you first need to identify the URL pattern or the specific HTML element that controls pagination.

For example, on many e-commerce websites, you might see a "Next" button or a series of page numbers that are wrapped in <a> tags. Here's an example of a pagination structure:

```html
Edit
<div class="pagination">
    <a href="/page/1">1</a>
    <a href="/page/2">2</a>
    <a href="/page/3">3</a>
    <a href="/page/4">Next</a>
</div>
```

To scrape multiple pages, we need to loop through the URLs and extract data from each page.

Using Loops for Scraping Multiple Pages

The next step is to use loops to iterate through each page, collect the desired data, and handle the pagination logic. We will use requests to fetch the page and BeautifulSoup to parse and extract the content.

1. **Basic Looping through Pages:** If the website has simple pagination, such as /page/1, /page/2, etc., you can construct the URLs dynamically and use a loop to scrape data from each page. Here's an example:

```python
Edit
import requests
from bs4 import BeautifulSoup

base_url                                    =
'https://example.com/products/page/'

# Number of pages to scrape
num_pages = 5

for page_num in range(1, num_pages + 1):
    url = f'{base_url}{page_num}'
    response = requests.get(url)
    soup   =   BeautifulSoup(response.text,
'html.parser')

    # Extract product names (for example)
    product_names   =   soup.find_all('h2',
class_='product-name')
    for name in product_names:
```

```
print(name.text)
```

In this example:

- o We loop through pages 1 to 5 by dynamically changing the `page_num` in the URL.
- o We scrape the product names from each page and print them.

2. **Handling Dynamic Pagination:** Some websites use JavaScript to load the next set of results dynamically (e.g., through a "Load More" button). In such cases, you might need to use **Selenium** or **requests-HTML** to interact with the page dynamically. We'll discuss using Selenium in later chapters for handling such dynamic content.

Real-world Example: Scraping Product Listings Across Multiple Pages

Let's say we want to scrape product listings from an e-commerce website that paginates its products across multiple pages. Here's how you can set up a scraper to navigate through these pages and gather product details.

Consider the following webpage structure where each product is contained within a `<div>` tag with the class `product-item`.

Each page of products is numbered, and the page URL changes like this: `/products?page=1`, `/products?page=2`, and so on.

```python
Edit
import requests
from bs4 import BeautifulSoup

base_url = 'https://example.com/products?page='
num_pages = 10  # Let's assume there are 10 pages
of products

for page_num in range(1, num_pages + 1):
    url = f'{base_url}{page_num}'
    response = requests.get(url)
    soup       =       BeautifulSoup(response.text,
'html.parser')

    # Extract product names, prices, and links
    product_items       =       soup.find_all('div',
class_='product-item')

    for item in product_items:
        product_name       =       item.find('h2',
class_='product-name').text
        price       =       item.find('span',
class_='price').text
        product_link       =       item.find('a',
class_='product-link')['href']
```

```
print(f'Product: {product_name}')
print(f'Price: {price}')
print(f'Link: {product_link}')
print('-' * 30)
```

In this example:

- We dynamically build the URL for each page.
- We then use BeautifulSoup to parse each page and extract the product name, price, and link.
- We print the extracted information for each product on each page.

This is a basic implementation of scraping multiple pages. It can be expanded to scrape additional data types, handle errors, and store results in a file (CSV, JSON, etc.).

Handling URL Patterns in Pagination

Pagination URLs often follow a predictable pattern, as seen in the example above where the page number is simply appended to the URL (e.g., `/page/1`, `/page/2`). Sometimes, pagination follows different patterns, such as using query parameters or paths.

1. **Query Parameter Pagination:** For example, the URL might look like `/products?page=1`,

/products?page=2, and so on. You can easily manage this pattern by looping through the numbers:

```python
Edit
base_url                                    =
'https://example.com/products?page='
num_pages = 10

for page_num in range(1, num_pages + 1):
    url = f'{base_url}{page_num}'
    # Continue scraping as before...
```

2. **Incremental Pagination (Path-based):** Some websites may have URLs like /products/page1, /products/page2, etc. In this case, you would simply increment the number in the path:

```python
Edit
base_url                                    =
'https://example.com/products/page'
num_pages = 10

for page_num in range(1, num_pages + 1):
    url = f'{base_url}{page_num}'
    # Continue scraping as before...
```

3. **Using the "Next" Button for Pagination:** Some websites use a "Next" button to navigate between pages. You can programmatically find the "Next" button and follow the link to the next page. This requires inspecting the page to locate the "Next" button or link.

Example of scraping with a "Next" button:

```python
Edit
url = 'https://example.com/products'
while url:
    response = requests.get(url)
    soup = BeautifulSoup(response.text,
'html.parser')

    # Scrape product details...

    # Find the "Next" button link
    next_button       =       soup.find('a',
class_='next')
    if next_button:
        url = next_button.get('href')
    else:
        break  # No more pages
```

In this case, we follow the link to the "Next" page by inspecting the <a> tag with the class next. If no "Next" button exists, we break out of the loop.

Conclusion of Chapter 8

Scraping multiple pages is a common and vital task in web scraping. By handling pagination, loops, and URL patterns, you can efficiently scrape large datasets spread across multiple pages. Whether dealing with simple page numbers or more complex "Next" buttons, the tools discussed in this chapter provide a solid foundation for scraping multiple pages effectively.

With this knowledge, you'll be able to extend your scraper to handle paginated data sources and collect comprehensive datasets for analysis.

CHAPTER 9

STORING SCRAPED DATA

One of the key steps in web scraping is storing the data you've collected in a useful format. Whether you are scraping product listings, blog posts, or financial data, it's essential to save the information in a structured format for further analysis, reporting, or even as a dataset for machine learning.

In this chapter, we will discuss various methods for storing scraped data. We'll look at CSV, JSON, and database options (SQLite and MySQL), providing practical examples for each. Understanding how to efficiently store your data is crucial for both small-scale and large-scale scraping projects.

Storing Data in CSV Format

CSV (Comma Separated Values) is one of the most common and simplest formats to store scraped data. CSV files are human-readable and easy to import into software like Excel, Google Sheets, or data analysis tools like pandas.

1. **Why Use CSV?**
    - Simple and widely supported.
    - Easy to open in spreadsheet software.

o Works well for smaller datasets.

2. **How to Write Data to a CSV File:**

Python's built-in `csv` module provides easy functionality to write data into a CSV file. Let's assume we are scraping product data from an e-commerce site, and we want to store the product name, price, and link in a CSV file.

Example:

```python
Edit
import csv
import requests
from bs4 import BeautifulSoup

base_url                                    =
'https://example.com/products?page='
num_pages = 5
data = []

for page_num in range(1, num_pages + 1):
    url = f'{base_url}{page_num}'
    response = requests.get(url)
    soup  =  BeautifulSoup(response.text,
'html.parser')

    # Extracting product data
```

```
    product_items = soup.find_all('div',
class_='product-item')
    for item in product_items:
        product_name = item.find('h2',
class_='product-name').text.strip()
        price = item.find('span',
class_='price').text.strip()
        product_link = item.find('a',
class_='product-link')['href']

        data.append([product_name, price,
product_link])

# Writing to a CSV file
with open('products.csv', mode='w',
newline='', encoding='utf-8') as file:
    writer = csv.writer(file)
    writer.writerow(['Product      Name',
'Price', 'Link'])  # Writing header
    writer.writerows(data)
```

Explanation:

- We iterate through the pages and extract product data.
- The csv.writer is used to write the headers and rows of product data into a CSV file.
- The newline='' ensures there are no extra blank lines between rows.

3. **Advantages of CSV:**

   o Easy to understand and use.

   o Perfect for small projects or quick prototyping.

Writing Data to JSON Files

JSON (JavaScript Object Notation) is another popular data storage format, particularly when dealing with nested or hierarchical data. JSON is widely used in APIs and web services because of its ease of use and lightweight structure.

1. **Why Use JSON?**

   o Ideal for complex data structures (like lists of dictionaries).

   o Widely supported in web development and APIs.

   o Easy to work with in programming languages like Python.

2. **How to Write Data to a JSON File:**

   Python provides a built-in `json` module that allows you to easily write data to a JSON file. Let's say we're scraping product data and want to store it in a structured JSON format.

   Example:

   ```python
   python
   ```

91

```
Edit
import json
import requests
from bs4 import BeautifulSoup

base_url                                    =
'https://example.com/products?page='
num_pages = 5
product_data = []

for page_num in range(1, num_pages + 1):
    url = f'{base_url}{page_num}'
    response = requests.get(url)
    soup  =  BeautifulSoup(response.text,
'html.parser')

    # Extract product data
    product_items  =  soup.find_all('div',
class_='product-item')
    for item in product_items:
        product = {
            'name':          item.find('h2',
class_='product-name').text.strip(),
            'price':      item.find('span',
class_='price').text.strip(),
            'link':          item.find('a',
class_='product-link')['href']
        }
        product_data.append(product)
```

92

```
# Writing to a JSON file
with       open('products.json',       'w',
encoding='utf-8') as json_file:
    json.dump(product_data,      json_file,
ensure_ascii=False, indent=4)
```

Explanation:

- We store the scraped data in a dictionary for each product.
- The `json.dump()` function writes the `product_data` list (containing dictionaries) to a JSON file.
- The `ensure_ascii=False` option ensures that non-ASCII characters are written correctly, and `indent=4` formats the JSON output for readability.

3. **Advantages of JSON:**
   - Handles complex or nested data structures well.
   - Lightweight and easy to work with in modern web applications.

Storing Data in Databases

When dealing with large datasets or more complex projects, storing your scraped data in a database is a more efficient and scalable approach. Databases provide powerful query capabilities, indexing, and the ability to store vast amounts of data. Python's support for databases makes it easy to interact with popular relational database systems like SQLite and MySQL.

SQLite is a lightweight, file-based relational database that is easy to use and doesn't require a server setup.

1. **Why Use SQLite?**
   - o Ideal for smaller, local applications.
   - o File-based database, meaning no need to install or configure a database server.
   - o Supports SQL queries for data manipulation.
2. **How to Store Data in SQLite:**

   Example:

```python
Edit
import sqlite3
import requests
from bs4 import BeautifulSoup

# Create SQLite database and table
conn = sqlite3.connect('products.db')
cursor = conn.cursor()
```

```python
cursor.execute('''CREATE    TABLE    IF    NOT
EXISTS products
                    (name TEXT, price TEXT,
link TEXT)''')

base_url                              =
'https://example.com/products?page='
num_pages = 5

for page_num in range(1, num_pages + 1):
    url = f'{base_url}{page_num}'
    response = requests.get(url)
    soup    =    BeautifulSoup(response.text,
'html.parser')

    # Extract product data
    product_items    =    soup.find_all('div',
class_='product-item')
    for item in product_items:
        product_name    =    item.find('h2',
class_='product-name').text.strip()
        price    =    item.find('span',
class_='price').text.strip()
        product_link    =    item.find('a',
class_='product-link')['href']

        # Insert data into SQLite database
```

```
        cursor.execute('INSERT        INTO
products (name, price, link) VALUES (?, ?,
?)',
                        (product_name,
price, product_link))

# Commit and close the database connection
conn.commit()
conn.close()
```

Explanation:

- o We create an SQLite database and a `products` table to store the data.
- o For each product, we insert the data into the table using SQL `INSERT` queries.

Using MySQL:

For larger projects, MySQL or other relational databases offer better performance and scalability. MySQL is a powerful, server-based database that supports larger datasets and can handle more complex queries.

1. **Why Use MySQL?**
   - o Designed for large-scale, high-performance applications.
   - o Supports complex SQL queries and transactions.

o Requires a server setup but is highly scalable.

2. **How to Store Data in MySQL:**

Example:

```python
Edit
import mysql.connector
import requests
from bs4 import BeautifulSoup

# Connect to MySQL database
conn = mysql.connector.connect(
    host="localhost",        user="root",
password="your_password",
database="scraping_db"
)
cursor = conn.cursor()

# Create table if it doesn't exist
cursor.execute('''CREATE   TABLE   IF   NOT
EXISTS products
                (name       VARCHAR(255),
price VARCHAR(100), link TEXT)''')

base_url                                    =
'https://example.com/products?page='
num_pages = 5
```

```python
for page_num in range(1, num_pages + 1):
    url = f'{base_url}{page_num}'
    response = requests.get(url)
    soup  =  BeautifulSoup(response.text,
'html.parser')

    # Extract product data
    product_items  =  soup.find_all('div',
class_='product-item')
    for item in product_items:
        product_name  =  item.find('h2',
class_='product-name').text.strip()
        price  =  item.find('span',
class_='price').text.strip()
        product_link  =  item.find('a',
class_='product-link')['href']

        # Insert data into MySQL database
        cursor.execute('INSERT      INTO
products (name, price, link) VALUES (%s,
%s, %s)',
                        (product_name,
price, product_link))

# Commit and close the connection
conn.commit()
conn.close()
```

Explanation:

- o We connect to the MySQL server and create a table to store product information.
- o We insert product data into the database using SQL INSERT statements.

Conclusion of Chapter 9

Choosing the right storage format for your scraped data depends on the scale of your project and how you plan to use the data. CSV is great for smaller datasets or when quick access is needed, while JSON offers a flexible way to store more complex data. For larger datasets or applications requiring advanced querying, relational databases like SQLite and MySQL are the way to go.

By mastering data storage techniques, you can ensure that your web scraping projects scale effectively and your data is well-organized for further analysis.

CHAPTER 10

HANDLING ERRORS AND EXCEPTIONS

In any web scraping project, dealing with errors and exceptions is an inevitable part of the process. Websites may change, elements might be missing, network conditions can fluctuate, and data may not always be in the expected format. It's crucial to handle these errors effectively to ensure your scraper doesn't break down unexpectedly and continues to run smoothly.

In this chapter, we'll walk through common errors during scraping, how to handle exceptions in Python, and best practices to build robust scrapers that can handle issues like timeouts, broken links, and unexpected data formats.

Common Errors During Scraping

There are several types of errors that are commonly encountered while web scraping. Understanding these errors will help you prepare your code to handle them properly.

1. **Network-Related Errors:**

- o **Timeouts:** The connection to the server might take longer than expected, causing a timeout error. This can happen due to slow internet connections or server-side issues.
- o **Connection Errors:** Sometimes the server is unreachable, which can lead to connection errors.
- o **Request Failures (HTTP Errors):** The server might return an error status code (e.g., 404 for "Not Found", 503 for "Service Unavailable").

2. **Parsing Errors:**
   - o **Missing Elements:** The web page structure might have changed, or an element you are trying to scrape might be missing.
   - o **Malformed HTML:** Scraping a page with poorly structured HTML can result in parsing errors.

3. **Unexpected Data:**
   - o **Data Type Mismatches:** Your code might expect text, but the data could be an image or a file.
   - o **Empty or Incomplete Data:** Sometimes the data might not be fully available, leaving empty or incomplete fields.

Exception Handling in Python

Python provides a powerful mechanism to handle errors using try, except, else, and finally blocks. This allows you to gracefully manage errors and prevent your program from crashing when something goes wrong.

1. **Basic Exception Handling Structure:**

```python
Edit
try:
    # Code that might raise an error
    result = 10 / 0  # Division by zero
(example of an error)
except ZeroDivisionError as e:
    # Code to run if an error occurs
    print(f"Error occurred: {e}")
else:
    # Code to run if no error occurs
    print("No error occurred!")
finally:
    # Code to run regardless of whether an
error occurred or not
    print("This will always be printed.")
```

2. **Handling Specific Exceptions:**

When handling errors, it's best to be specific about the type of error you want to catch. Python has a range of built-in exceptions you can handle, including `ValueError`, `IndexError`, `KeyError`, and `TimeoutError`.

How to Handle Timeouts, Broken Links, and Unexpected Data Formats

Web scraping often involves interacting with unreliable web pages, which might be slow to load or have broken links. It's essential to handle these conditions appropriately to avoid your scraper failing unexpectedly.

1. **Handling Timeouts:**

   When making requests to a website, timeouts can happen if the server doesn't respond in a reasonable time. To handle this, you can set a timeout period for your requests and handle the `requests.exceptions.Timeout` exception.

   Example:

```python
Edit
import requests
```

```
try:
    response                           =
requests.get('https://example.com',
timeout=5)  # Timeout after 5 seconds
except requests.exceptions.Timeout:
    print("The request timed out. Please
try again later.")
```

Explanation:

- o   `timeout=5` sets the request to timeout after 5 seconds.
- o   If the request takes longer than that, it raises a `Timeout` exception, which is caught and handled.

2. **Handling Broken Links:**

Broken links often result in an HTTP error response, such as a 404 (Page Not Found) or 500 (Server Error). Using the `requests` library, you can check the HTTP status code of a response and handle different types of errors accordingly.

Example:

```
python
Edit
try:
```

```
    response                            =
requests.get('https://example.com/nonexis
tent-page')
    if response.status_code == 404:
        print("Page not found (404 error).
Skipping this link.")
except
requests.exceptions.RequestException as e:
    print(f"An error occurred: {e}")
```

Explanation:

- o   If the response returns a 404 status code, the code informs the user and skips scraping that link.
- o   `requests.exceptions.RequestExceptio n` is a general exception that catches all request-related errors.

3. **Handling Unexpected Data Formats:**

Sometimes, the data you scrape might not match the format you expect. For example, a tag might be missing or the content might be in an unexpected format (like a number where text is expected). You can use `try-except` blocks to handle such cases.

Example:

```
python
Edit
```

```
try:
    price          =          item.find('span',
class_='price').text.strip()
    price    =    float(price.replace('$',
'').replace(',', ''))   # Converting price
to float
except ValueError:
    print("Price   format   is   incorrect.
Skipping this item.")
    price = None   # Assigning None if the
price is invalid
```

Explanation:

- o In this case, the code expects the price to be a numeric value. If the value cannot be converted to a float (e.g., the data is in a different format), it catches the `ValueError` and prints an error message while continuing the loop.

Real-World Example: Building a Scraper That Handles Errors Gracefully

Let's take a closer look at how to build a robust scraper that handles errors, timeouts, broken links, and missing data. We'll scrape a simple e-commerce website that lists products and prices.

1. **Building the Scraper:**

```python
Edit
import requests
from bs4 import BeautifulSoup

base_url                              =
'https://example.com/products?page='
num_pages = 5
product_data = []

for page_num in range(1, num_pages + 1):
    url = f'{base_url}{page_num}'

    try:
        response    =    requests.get(url,
timeout=10)
        response.raise_for_status()       #
Raise HTTPError for bad responses
    except requests.exceptions.Timeout:
        print(f"Timeout   error   on   page
{page_num}. Retrying...")
        continue
    except
requests.exceptions.RequestException as e:
        print(f"Error  on  page  {page_num}:
{e}")
        continue
```

```python
    soup = BeautifulSoup(response.text,
'html.parser')

    # Extract product data
    product_items = soup.find_all('div',
class_='product-item')
    for item in product_items:
        try:
            product_name = item.find('h2',
class_='product-name').text.strip()
            price = item.find('span',
class_='price').text.strip()
            product_link = item.find('a',
class_='product-link')['href']
            price =
float(price.replace('$', '').replace(',',
''))  # Convert to float
        except (AttributeError,
ValueError) as e:
            print(f"Skipping item due to
error: {e}")
            continue

        product_data.append({
            'name': product_name,
            'price': price,
            'link': product_link
        })
```

```
print(f"Scraped data: {product_data}")
```

2. **Explanation of the Scraper:**

   o **Timeout Handling:** The scraper sets a timeout of 10 seconds for each request. If the server takes longer than that, it retries the request.

   o **Error Handling for HTTP Requests:** If there's any other issue with the request (e.g., 404 or 503), the scraper catches the `RequestException` and skips that page.

   o **Error Handling for Data Extraction:** If any product data is missing (e.g., missing price or product name), the scraper catches the `AttributeError` or `ValueError` and continues to the next product.

Best Practices for Error Handling in Web Scraping

- **Retry Logic:** Implement retry mechanisms when encountering temporary errors (like timeouts or server errors).
- **Logging:** Use Python's `logging` module to keep track of errors, which can help debug issues later.
- **Graceful Skipping:** Instead of stopping the entire scraper when an error occurs, skip the problematic item and continue scraping.

- **Rate Limiting and Politeness:** Avoid overwhelming a server with requests by respecting `robots.txt`, using polite scraping techniques, and adding delays between requests.

Conclusion of Chapter 10

By handling errors and exceptions effectively, you can create web scrapers that are more resilient and reliable, even when things don't go according to plan. Python's robust exception handling features, combined with thoughtful error management, allow you to scrape data without worrying about unexpected issues causing the scraper to crash. The techniques learned in this chapter will help you build scrapers that are both efficient and user-friendly, ensuring that you collect valuable data from the web while handling any challenges along the way.

CHAPTER 11

WEB SCRAPING WITH REQUESTS LIBRARY

In this chapter, we will dive into one of the most essential tools for web scraping in Python—the **Requests library**. It is one of the most popular libraries for sending HTTP requests, including GET and POST requests, which is crucial for extracting data from web pages. By the end of this chapter, you will have a solid understanding of how to use Requests in combination with BeautifulSoup to scrape data from a website.

Introduction to the Requests Library

The **Requests** library is a simple, yet powerful, HTTP library for Python that allows you to send HTTP requests with ease. Whether you're scraping a static page, submitting a form, or handling headers and cookies, the Requests library simplifies these tasks.

Unlike the built-in `urllib` library, which can be somewhat cumbersome for simple web scraping tasks, **Requests** is designed to be intuitive and user-friendly, making it the go-to library for sending HTTP requests in Python.

111

To get started, you first need to install the library, which you can do via pip:

```bash
Edit
pip install requests
```

Once installed, you can start sending HTTP requests to a website.

Making HTTP Requests (GET, POST)

The primary action in web scraping is making HTTP requests to retrieve the content of a webpage. You can do this with **GET** requests for retrieving data, and **POST** requests for submitting data (such as forms or search queries).

1. **GET Request:** A **GET** request is used to request data from a specified resource. It's the most common method for retrieving HTML pages.

   Example:

   ```python
   Edit
   import requests

   url = 'https://example.com'
   response = requests.get(url)
   ```

```
# Check if the request was successful
if response.status_code == 200:
    print("Successfully    fetched    the
webpage!")
    print(response.text)  # HTML content of
the page
else:
    print(f"Failed    to    retrieve    the
webpage.         Status              code:
{response.status_code}")
```

In this example, we use `requests.get()` to fetch the content of the page at `https://example.com`. The `response` object contains all the information about the response, including the HTML content of the page in `response.text`.

2. **POST Request:** A **POST** request is used to submit data to a server. It's often used when you need to submit forms or perform searches. You can send data in the form of parameters, such as form data or JSON.

Example:

```python
Edit
import requests
```

```
url = 'https://example.com/search'
data = {'query': 'python web scraping'}
response = requests.post(url, data=data)

if response.status_code == 200:
    print("Successfully posted the data!")
    print(response.text)
else:
    print(f"Failed to post the data. Status
code: {response.status_code}")
```

Here, we are using `requests.post()` to send form data
(`query: python web scraping`) to the server. This
is often used for submitting search queries or other user
inputs.

Handling Query Parameters and Headers

Many websites expect specific query parameters and headers to
be passed in HTTP requests. This is especially important when
interacting with APIs or when you want to simulate a real user
browsing the web (i.e., including headers that make the request
appear as though it's from a browser).

1. **Query Parameters:**

Query parameters are typically used in GET requests to send data to the server in the URL. These are often used for things like search terms or filters.

Example:

```python
Edit
import requests

url = 'https://example.com/search'
params = {'query': 'python web scraping',
'page': 1}
response         =         requests.get(url,
params=params)

if response.status_code == 200:
    print("Successfully   retrieved   data
with query parameters!")
    print(response.text)
else:
    print(f"Failed   to   retrieve   data.
Status code: {response.status_code}")
```

In this case, the `params` dictionary contains the query parameters `query` and `page`, which are automatically encoded into the URL by the `requests.get()` method.

2. **Headers:**

115

Some websites require specific headers (such as User-Agent) to be set in requests to simulate a real browser request. You can send custom headers using the headers parameter in the requests method.

Example:

```python
Edit
import requests

url = 'https://example.com'
headers = {'User-Agent': 'Mozilla/5.0
(Windows NT 10.0; Win64; x64)
AppleWebKit/537.36 (KHTML, like Gecko)
Chrome/91.0.4472.124 Safari/537.36'}
response = requests.get(url,
headers=headers)

if response.status_code == 200:
    print("Successfully fetched the
webpage with custom headers!")
    print(response.text)
else:
    print(f"Failed to retrieve the
webpage. Status code:
{response.status_code}")
```

Here, we are sending a custom **User-Agent** header to mimic a request from a Chrome browser. Some websites block requests that don't have a valid User-Agent header, so including this can help bypass such restrictions.

Practical Example: Scraping a Website with Requests and BeautifulSoup

Now that you know how to make HTTP requests and handle query parameters and headers, let's see how to combine **Requests** with **BeautifulSoup** to scrape data from a webpage. In this example, we'll scrape a fictional blog's homepage to collect article titles.

1. **Code Example:**

```python
Edit
import requests
from bs4 import BeautifulSoup

url = 'https://example-blog.com'
headers = {'User-Agent': 'Mozilla/5.0
(Windows NT 10.0; Win64; x64)
AppleWebKit/537.36 (KHTML, like Gecko)
Chrome/91.0.4472.124 Safari/537.36'}
response = requests.get(url,
headers=headers)
```

117

```python
if response.status_code == 200:
    print("Successfully fetched the blog
page!")

    # Parse the content with BeautifulSoup
    soup = BeautifulSoup(response.text,
'html.parser')

    # Find all article titles
    articles = soup.find_all('h2',
class_='article-title')
    for article in articles:
        print(article.text.strip())        #
Output article titles
else:
    print(f"Failed to retrieve the
webpage. Status code:
{response.status_code}")
```

2. **Explanation:**

   o   We start by sending a GET request to the URL of
       the blog's homepage. The `User-Agent` header is
       included to simulate a real browser request.

   o   After getting the response, we use **BeautifulSoup**
       to parse the HTML content of the page
       (`response.text`).

118

o   We then use BeautifulSoup's `find_all()` method to find all the article titles by searching for `<h2>` tags with the class `article-title`.

o   Finally, we loop through the list of articles and print out the text of each title.

Conclusion of Chapter 11

By now, you should be familiar with how to use the **Requests library** for making HTTP requests and how to handle query parameters and custom headers. Using **Requests** in combination with **BeautifulSoup** allows you to efficiently scrape static content from websites and extract the data you need.

In this chapter, we covered:

- Making GET and POST requests.
- Handling query parameters and headers for more complex requests.
- A practical example of scraping data with **Requests** and **BeautifulSoup**.

With this knowledge, you can start scraping websites and extracting data effectively. In the next chapters, we will dive deeper into handling dynamic content, advanced scraping techniques, and organizing the data you collect.

CHAPTER 12

AUTOMATING WEB SCRAPING

In this chapter, we'll explore how to automate your web scraping tasks. Automation can save time and effort by enabling your scrapers to run periodically, ensuring you collect fresh data at regular intervals without manual intervention. Whether you're gathering financial data, news updates, or product listings, automating your scraping tasks will help streamline your workflow. By the end of this chapter, you'll know how to schedule your scraping jobs and build a simple automation pipeline for continuous data collection.

Automating Periodic Scraping Tasks

Automating web scraping tasks is useful when you need to collect data on a regular basis, such as pulling stock prices daily or scraping product prices from an e-commerce site every hour. There are several ways to automate web scraping jobs, but the most common methods involve scheduling tasks using system tools like **Cron** (on Linux-based systems) or **Task Scheduler** (on Windows).

1. **Why Automate?** Automating your web scraping tasks allows you to:

   o Collect fresh data without needing to run scripts manually.

   o Schedule scraping jobs during off-peak hours to reduce the load on both your system and the target website.

   o Ensure continuous data collection, even when you are away from the computer.

2. **How to Automate:** To automate scraping tasks, you will need a way to:

   o Write a script to perform the scraping task.

   o Schedule the script to run periodically (e.g., every hour, every day, etc.).

Scheduling Scrapers with Cron Jobs (Linux)

Cron is a time-based job scheduler in Unix-like operating systems, including Linux. It allows you to run tasks at specific intervals (e.g., daily, weekly, hourly). Here's how you can use Cron to schedule a web scraping script:

1. **Writing the Scraping Script:** First, ensure you have a Python script that performs the scraping task. For example, let's say you want to scrape stock prices from a

financial website. You can create a Python script called `scrape_stock_prices.py` with the following content:

```python
Edit
import requests
from bs4 import BeautifulSoup

# Scraping stock prices (Example)
url = 'https://example.com/stock-prices'
response = requests.get(url)
soup    =    BeautifulSoup(response.text,
'html.parser')
stock_prices    =    soup.find_all('span',
class_='price')

# Saving data to a file
with open('stock_prices.txt', 'a') as f:
    for price in stock_prices:
        f.write(price.text.strip() + '\n')

print("Stock prices scraped and saved!")
```

2. **Setting Up the Cron Job:** To run this script at a regular interval, we need to add it to the **Cron** scheduler. Open your terminal and run the following command:

```bash
Edit
```

```
crontab -e
```

This will open the cron table in an editor. Add a line to schedule the script. For example, to run the script every day at 9 AM, add the following line:

```
ruby
Edit
0    9    *    *    *    /usr/bin/python3
/path/to/scrape_stock_prices.py
```

- o   0 9 * * * indicates the schedule (run at 9 AM every day).
- o   /usr/bin/python3 is the path to Python on your system.
- o   /path/to/scrape_stock_prices.py is the full path to your Python script.

3. **Testing the Cron Job:** To ensure your cron job is working, check the file where the data is stored (in this case, stock_prices.txt). If the script runs as scheduled, the file should be updated with the latest stock prices at 9 AM each day.

Scheduling Scrapers with Task Scheduler (Windows)

Windows offers a built-in utility called **Task Scheduler**, which allows you to run tasks on a schedule. Here's how you can use Task Scheduler to automate your scraping script:

1. **Writing the Scraping Script:** As with the Cron job, start by ensuring your scraping script is working as expected. The Python script should perform the scraping task (such as collecting stock prices) and save the results to a file.

2. **Setting Up Task Scheduler:** To schedule the script, follow these steps:

    o   Open the **Task Scheduler** application (search for "Task Scheduler" in the Start menu).

    o   In the **Actions** pane, click **Create Basic Task**.

    o   Provide a name and description for the task (e.g., "Scrape Stock Prices").

    o   Choose **Daily**, **Weekly**, or any other frequency you want for the task.

    o   For **Action**, choose **Start a Program**, and in the **Program/script** field, browse to your Python executable (typically found at `C:\Python\Python3x\python.exe`).

    o   In the **Add arguments** field, enter the path to your script, for example:

    vbnet

```
Edit
C:\path\to\scrape_stock_prices.py
```

- o Finish the wizard, and your script will now run on the schedule you've set.

3. **Testing the Scheduled Task:** After setting up the task, right-click it in Task Scheduler and choose **Run** to test if the script executes correctly. Check the output file (e.g., stock_prices.txt) to ensure the data is saved.

Building a Simple Scraping Automation Pipeline

Now that you know how to automate web scraping tasks, let's discuss how you can build a basic automation pipeline that performs the following:

- Scrapes data from a target website.
- Saves the data to a file (CSV, JSON, etc.).
- Notifies you when the task is complete.

1. **Pipeline Overview:** The pipeline can consist of the following steps:
   - o **Scrape Data:** Use BeautifulSoup and Requests to extract the data from a website.
   - o **Process Data:** Clean, transform, or analyze the scraped data as necessary.

- o **Save Data:** Store the processed data in a file (e.g., CSV, JSON) or database.
- o **Notify User:** Send an email or other notification when the scraping task is complete.

2. **Code Example (Scraping Stock Prices):** Let's build a simple pipeline that scrapes stock prices, saves the data to a CSV file, and sends an email notification when the task is complete.

```python
Edit
import requests
import csv
from bs4 import BeautifulSoup
from smtplib import SMTP


def scrape_stock_prices():
    url = 'https://example.com/stock-
prices'
    response = requests.get(url)
    soup = BeautifulSoup(response.text,
'html.parser')
    stock_prices = soup.find_all('span',
class_='price')


    with open('stock_prices.csv', 'a',
newline='') as csvfile:
        writer = csv.writer(csvfile)
        for price in stock_prices:
```

```
writer.writerow([price.text.strip()])

    print("Stock    prices    scraped    and
saved!")

def send_notification():
    server = SMTP('smtp.gmail.com', 587)
    server.starttls()
    server.login('your-
email@example.com', 'your-email-password')
    message = "Subject: Scraping Task
Completed\n\nThe stock price scraping task
has completed successfully."
    server.sendmail('your-
email@example.com',              'recipient-
email@example.com', message)
    server.quit()
    print("Notification sent!")

if __name__ == "__main__":
    scrape_stock_prices()
    send_notification()
```

In this example:

o **scrape_stock_prices()**: Scrapes the stock
    prices and saves them to a CSV file.

127

- ○ **send_notification()**: Sends an email notification when the task is completed.
3. **Scheduling the Pipeline:** Once the script is working, you can automate this pipeline by scheduling it using Cron (Linux) or Task Scheduler (Windows), as discussed earlier.

Real-World Example: Automating Data Collection for Stock Prices

To illustrate the practical use of automation, imagine you want to automate the collection of stock prices from a financial website every hour. By using the methods outlined above, you can set up a Cron job (or Task Scheduler task) to run your scraping script every hour. The script would automatically fetch the latest stock prices, save them to a CSV file, and even send you an email when the task completes.

This automated data collection can then be used for further analysis, building financial models, or simply tracking price trends over time.

Conclusion of Chapter 12

In this chapter, we have covered how to automate web scraping tasks using Cron jobs on Linux and Task Scheduler on Windows.

We also discussed how to build a simple web scraping automation pipeline and a real-world example of automating data collection for stock prices.

Automating web scraping allows you to:

- Collect fresh data at regular intervals.
- Eliminate the need for manual intervention.
- Ensure consistent data collection without error.

With the knowledge from this chapter, you can now set up and manage automated scraping tasks, saving time and resources. In the next chapters, we will discuss more advanced automation techniques, error handling, and optimizing your scraping pipeline for large-scale data collection.

CHAPTER 13

WEB SCRAPING WITH APIS

In this chapter, we'll explore the powerful world of **APIs (Application Programming Interfaces)** and how they can be used in web scraping. APIs provide a structured and efficient way to retrieve data directly from a website or service, often bypassing the need to scrape raw HTML content. We will discuss the advantages of using APIs over traditional scraping methods, how to access data via REST APIs using Python, and how to handle API responses.

By the end of this chapter, you'll understand the role of APIs in modern web scraping workflows and how to integrate API data into your scraping projects.

Introduction to APIs and Their Advantages Over Web Scraping

Before diving into coding, let's start by understanding what an API is and why it's often a better option than traditional web scraping.

1. **What is an API?** An API is a set of protocols and tools for building software applications. APIs allow different systems to communicate with each other. In the context of web scraping, many websites and services expose APIs

130

that allow users to request data in a structured format, typically JSON or XML, without needing to scrape HTML pages directly.

2. **Advantages of Using APIs Over Web Scraping:**
   - o **Efficiency:** APIs are designed to return the data you need in a structured format, making it easier to process than raw HTML content.
   - o **Reliability:** Since APIs are meant to provide data directly, they are generally more stable and less prone to changes than web page structures.
   - o **Legality and Ethics:** Many websites offer APIs with clear usage guidelines, reducing the ethical and legal concerns associated with scraping HTML.
   - o **Rate Limits and Authentication:** APIs often have built-in rate limits to control how many requests can be made within a given time frame, ensuring fair use of the service.

3. **When to Use an API vs. Scraping:**
   - o **Use an API** when the website explicitly offers an API that provides the data you're looking for in a structured format.
   - o **Use web scraping** when the website doesn't offer an API or if the API doesn't provide the data you need.

In this chapter, we'll focus on accessing and using **REST APIs**, which are one of the most common types of APIs for web scraping.

Using Python to Access REST APIs

A **REST API** (Representational State Transfer) is a popular type of API that communicates via HTTP requests and returns data in standard formats such as **JSON** or **XML**. Let's walk through how you can use Python to interact with a REST API.

1. **Making HTTP Requests with the `requests` Library:** Python's `requests` library is a great tool for making HTTP requests to interact with APIs. Here's how you can use it to make a request to a REST API.

   First, ensure that you have the `requests` library installed:

   ```bash
   Edit
   pip install requests
   ```

   Then, you can write a script to make a **GET** request to fetch data from an API:

   ```python
   ```

```
Edit
import requests

# API URL (Example: JSONPlaceholder API)
url                                        =
'https://jsonplaceholder.typicode.com/pos
ts'

# Making a GET request to the API
response = requests.get(url)

# Check if the request was successful
if response.status_code == 200:
    data = response.json()  # Convert the
response to JSON
    print(data)  # Print the data
else:
    print(f"Failed   to   retrieve   data:
{response.status_code}")
```

- o **requests.get()** sends a GET request to the API endpoint.
- o **response.json()** converts the JSON response into a Python dictionary for easy processing.

This is a simple example, but it demonstrates how to connect to an API and retrieve data in a structured format.

Converting API Responses to BeautifulSoup Objects

While REST APIs typically return structured data in JSON format, sometimes you might want to convert this data into an HTML-like format, especially if you're dealing with data that needs additional parsing. For this, we can use **BeautifulSoup**, which is mainly designed for parsing HTML.

1. **Why Convert API Responses?** In some cases, the raw JSON response from an API might contain HTML content as part of its fields, such as descriptions, blog posts, or comments. If you need to extract or clean specific HTML content embedded in the JSON response, you can use BeautifulSoup to parse it.

2. **Converting JSON to BeautifulSoup:** Once you have the API response, you can parse any HTML elements that might be present in the response using BeautifulSoup. Here's an example:

```python
Edit
import requests
from bs4 import BeautifulSoup

# API URL (Example: JSONPlaceholder API)
url                             =
'https://jsonplaceholder.typicode.com/pos
ts'
```

134

```python
# Making a GET request to the API
response = requests.get(url)

if response.status_code == 200:
    data = response.json()  # Convert the response to JSON

    # Suppose each post contains an HTML snippet that needs parsing
    for post in data:
        html_content = post['body'] # HTML content inside the post body
        soup = BeautifulSoup(html_content, 'html.parser')

        # Extract specific elements, e.g., the first paragraph
        first_paragraph = soup.find('p')
        print(f"First paragraph: {first_paragraph.text}")
else:
    print(f"Failed to retrieve data: {response.status_code}")
```

o **BeautifulSoup()** parses the html_content field from the API response.

○ **soup.find()** allows you to extract specific HTML elements (e.g., paragraphs, links) from the parsed HTML.

Real-World Example: Scraping Data from a Public API

Let's now look at a more concrete example: scraping data from a **public API**. In this case, we'll use the **JSONPlaceholder API**, which provides fake online data that can be used for testing and learning purposes. We'll scrape user information from the API and process the data.

1. **Accessing the API:** JSONPlaceholder provides various endpoints, including one for user data. Here's how to access the data from the /users endpoint.

```python
Edit
import requests

# JSONPlaceholder users API endpoint
url                                    =
'https://jsonplaceholder.typicode.com/use
rs'

# Sending a GET request
response = requests.get(url)
```

```python
if response.status_code == 200:
    users = response.json()  # Convert the
response to JSON

    # Loop through the users and print
their names and emails
    for user in users:
        print(f"Name:      {user['name']},
Email: {user['email']}")
else:
    print(f"Failed to retrieve data:
{response.status_code}")
```

In this example, we send a GET request to the `https://jsonplaceholder.typicode.com/user s` endpoint. The response is returned as a JSON array of user objects, each containing fields like `name`, `email`, and `address`. We loop through this data and print out the user's name and email.

2. **Handling More Complex APIs:** Some APIs require additional configuration, such as authentication (API keys, OAuth), query parameters, or pagination for large data sets. For instance, the GitHub API requires an access token to fetch user data. Always refer to the API documentation for specific instructions.

Conclusion of Chapter 13

In this chapter, we've learned how to interact with **REST APIs** in Python using the `requests` library. We've seen how to:

- Access APIs and retrieve structured data (usually JSON).
- Use **BeautifulSoup** to parse and extract information from HTML content within API responses.
- Work with a real-world example, scraping data from a public API like JSONPlaceholder.

By leveraging APIs for web scraping, you can streamline the process of data collection and avoid some of the challenges associated with scraping raw HTML. APIs provide a more reliable and efficient way to gather data from online services, and they often come with better documentation and support than scraping websites directly.

In the following chapters, we will dive deeper into advanced topics such as API authentication, error handling, and dealing with large data sets.

CHAPTER 14

HANDLING ANTI-SCRAPING MEASURES

Web scraping can be an incredibly powerful tool, but many websites actively work to prevent it. Websites use **anti-scraping measures** to protect their data and ensure the functionality of their site for real users. These measures can include techniques like CAPTCHAs, rate limiting, IP blocking, and user agent restrictions. In this chapter, we'll dive into common anti-scraping techniques, how to detect and bypass them, and how to use tools like proxies, headless browsers, and more to overcome these hurdles.

By the end of this chapter, you'll understand how to deal with these anti-scraping measures and continue scraping effectively while remaining ethical and respectful of website terms.

Detecting and Bypassing CAPTCHAs

A **CAPTCHA** (Completely Automated Public Turing test to tell Computers and Humans Apart) is one of the most common anti-scraping measures websites use. It's designed to differentiate between human users and automated bots. While CAPTCHAs

139

serve a legitimate purpose, they can be a barrier for web scrapers. There are various types of CAPTCHAs, such as text-based challenges, image recognition, and reCAPTCHA.

1. **Types of CAPTCHAs:**
    o **Text-based CAPTCHAs:** Users are asked to interpret and type distorted letters and numbers.
    o **Image-based CAPTCHAs:** Users are asked to select images that meet a specific criterion (e.g., "select all images with traffic lights").
    o **Invisible CAPTCHAs (reCAPTCHA v2/v3):** These detect bots based on user behavior (e.g., mouse movements, click patterns).

2. **Bypassing CAPTCHAs:** While solving CAPTCHAs manually is possible, it's not practical for large-scale scraping. Here's how to bypass or avoid CAPTCHAs:
    o **Third-Party CAPTCHA Solvers:**
        ▪ **2Captcha** and **AntiCaptcha** are paid services that allow you to send CAPTCHA images to real humans who solve them for you, returning the response that lets your script continue.
        ▪ Example using **2Captcha**:

```python
Edit
import requests
```

```python
import time

# Use the 2Captcha service to
solve the CAPTCHA
def solve_captcha(image_url):
    api_key                =
'your_2captcha_api_key'
    site_url               =
'https://example.com/captcha_
page'
    payload = {
        'method':
'userrecaptcha',
        'googlekey':
'site_key_from_page',
        'pageurl': site_url,
        'key': api_key,
    }
    response               =
requests.post('http://2captch
a.com/in.php', data=payload)
    captcha_id             =
response.text.split('|')[1]

    # Wait for the solution
    time.sleep(20)

    # Get the solved CAPTCHA
answer
```

```
    result                =
requests.get(f'http://2captch
a.com/res.php?key={api_key}&a
ction=get&id={captcha_id}')
    return
result.text.split('|')[1]


captcha_answer            =
solve_captcha('http://example
.com/captcha_image.jpg')
print(f"CAPTCHA      solved:
{captcha_answer}")
```

o **Headless Browsers:** Tools like **Selenium** and **Pyppeteer** can simulate human-like interaction with web pages, making it harder for CAPTCHAs to detect a bot.

Working with User Agents, Proxies, and IP Rotation

Websites often track your **IP address** and **user agent** to detect scraping behavior. If a website notices too many requests coming from the same IP or with the same user agent, it might block or throttle those requests. Let's look at how to work with **user agents, proxies**, and **IP rotation** to mitigate detection.

1. **Using User Agents:** The **user agent** string is a piece of data sent by your browser to identify itself to a website. It includes information such as the browser type, version, and operating system. By default, web scrapers often use Python's `requests` library or other tools with a default user agent that is easy for websites to identify as non-human.

   o **How to use custom user agents:** To mask your scraper's identity, you can change the user agent to mimic a real browser. This helps avoid detection.

   ```python
   Edit
   import requests

   headers = {
       'User-Agent': 'Mozilla/5.0
   (Windows NT 10.0; Win64; x64)
   AppleWebKit/537.36 (KHTML, like
   Gecko) Chrome/91.0.4472.124
   Safari/537.36'
   }

   response =
   requests.get('https://example.com',
   headers=headers)
   print(response.content)
   ```

2. **Using Proxies and IP Rotation:** If a website starts blocking your IP after repeated requests, you can **rotate IP addresses** to avoid this. Using **proxies** is a common technique for this.

   o **Rotating proxies** involves using a large pool of IP addresses that your scraper can switch between. There are several ways to set up proxy rotation:

      ▪ **Free proxy lists**: While these are available online, they are often unreliable and slow.

      ▪ **Paid proxy services**: Providers like **ProxyMesh**, **ScraperAPI**, or **Luminati** provide reliable proxy networks for web scraping.

   o **Using a proxy with requests**:

```python
Edit
proxies = {
    'http':
'http://your_proxy_ip:port',
    'https':
'https://your_proxy_ip:port',
}
```

```
response                        =
requests.get('https://example.com',
proxies=proxies)
print(response.content)
```

3. **Handling Proxy Rotation:** If you're using a pool of proxies, you can rotate through them programmatically. There are libraries available to make this easier, such as **requests-rotate** or **scrapy-rotating-proxies**.

```python
Edit
import random
import requests

proxies_list      =        ['http://proxy1',
'http://proxy2', 'http://proxy3']

# Randomly select a proxy
selected_proxy                              =
random.choice(proxies_list)

response                                    =
requests.get('https://example.com',
proxies={'http': selected_proxy, 'https':
selected_proxy})
print(response.content)
```

145

Using Headless Browsers (Selenium and Pyppeteer)

Sometimes websites use more advanced anti-scraping techniques, such as **JavaScript rendering**, which makes it harder to scrape with traditional libraries like `requests` or `BeautifulSoup`. In such cases, **headless browsers** like **Selenium** and **Pyppeteer** can simulate real user interactions, bypassing most anti-scraping defenses.

1. **Selenium:** Selenium is a popular tool for automating web browsers. It can be used to interact with web pages, click on buttons, fill out forms, and scrape dynamic content rendered by JavaScript.

    o   **Setting up Selenium with Chrome:** First, you'll need to install Selenium and the Chrome WebDriver:

    ```bash
    Edit
    pip install selenium
    ```

    Then, you can use Selenium to interact with a page:

    ```python
    Edit
    from selenium import webdriver
    ```

```
from      selenium.webdriver.common.by
import By

options = webdriver.ChromeOptions()
options.add_argument('--headless')
# Run browser in headless mode

driver                            =
webdriver.Chrome(options=options)

driver.get('https://example.com')

# Example: Scrape page title
page_title = driver.title
print(f"Page Title: {page_title}")

driver.quit()
```

2. **Pyppeteer: Pyppeteer** is a Python wrapper for **Puppeteer**, a Node.js library that controls headless Chrome. Pyppeteer can be used in a similar way to Selenium for automating browsing tasks.

   o **Using Pyppeteer:**

```
python
Edit
import asyncio
from pyppeteer import launch
```

```
async def main():
    browser       =       await
launch(headless=True)
    page = await browser.newPage()
    await
page.goto('https://example.com')

    # Get the page title
    title = await page.title()
    print(f"Page Title: {title}")

    await browser.close()

asyncio.get_event_loop().run_until_
complete(main())
```

Real-World Example: Handling CAPTCHAs and Rate-Limiting

Imagine you're scraping a website that uses CAPTCHA and rate-limiting to block bots. Here's how you can combine multiple techniques to bypass these defenses.

- **First, use a headless browser (Selenium) to render the page**.
- **Then, if you hit a CAPTCHA**, send it to a CAPTCHA-solving service (e.g., 2Captcha).
- **Finally, rotate IP addresses using a proxy pool** to avoid getting blocked by rate-limiting.

148

By using Selenium, a CAPTCHA solver, and proxies, you can successfully scrape even sites with advanced anti-scraping mechanisms.

Conclusion of Chapter 14

In this chapter, we've discussed how to handle common anti-scraping measures such as **CAPTCHAs, rate-limiting**, and **IP blocking**. We've covered techniques like:

- Detecting and bypassing CAPTCHAs.
- Using custom **user agents** and **proxies**.
- **Rotating IPs** to avoid detection.
- Using **headless browsers** like Selenium and Pyppeteer to bypass JavaScript protections.

Handling anti-scraping measures responsibly is crucial to maintaining ethical scraping practices. Always respect a website's **robots.txt** file and be mindful of legal constraints, especially when bypassing anti-scraping technologies.

In the next chapter, we'll explore **scraping large datasets efficiently**, including handling pagination, throttling requests, and optimizing performance for large-scale scraping projects.

CHAPTER 15

ADVANCED SCRAPING TECHNIQUES: REGULAR EXPRESSIONS

In web scraping, not all data is neatly organized or easily accessible. Often, the information you want to extract is hidden within text that doesn't follow a predictable pattern. This is where **regular expressions (regex)** come in handy. Regular expressions are a powerful tool for matching and extracting specific patterns from strings. In this chapter, we'll explore how to use regular expressions with BeautifulSoup to scrape more complex data, and show how they can be integrated with web scraping workflows to handle more advanced extraction tasks.

By the end of this chapter, you will have a solid understanding of regex and know how to use it in combination with BeautifulSoup to tackle complex scraping challenges.

Introduction to Regular Expressions (Regex)

A **regular expression** is a sequence of characters that defines a search pattern. It allows you to find and manipulate text by specifying patterns that can match specific strings. Regex is incredibly versatile, and it's widely used for searching, validating, and extracting data from text.

- **Basic Syntax:**
    - . (dot): Matches any single character except a newline.
    - \d: Matches any digit (0-9).
    - \D: Matches any non-digit character.
    - \w: Matches any alphanumeric character (letters and digits).
    - \W: Matches any non-alphanumeric character.
    - \s: Matches any whitespace character (spaces, tabs, newlines).
    - \S: Matches any non-whitespace character.
    - []: A set of characters to match any one of them.
    - ^: Anchors the pattern at the beginning of the string.
    - $: Anchors the pattern at the end of the string.
    - (): Groups patterns together.
    - |: Acts as a logical OR.
- **Example:** To match any email address, you might use a regular expression like this:

```
less
```

```
Edit
```

151

```
[a-zA-Z0-9._%+-]+@[a-zA-Z0-9.-]+\.[a-zA-
Z]{2,}
```

This regex matches typical email formats like `example@domain.com`.

Using Regex with BeautifulSoup

BeautifulSoup is great for parsing HTML and XML documents and navigating their structure, but sometimes the information you want isn't nicely encapsulated in specific HTML tags or attributes. This is where **regular expressions** can help. With BeautifulSoup, you can use regex to filter through tag content, such as extracting text patterns or searching for URLs, phone numbers, or other patterns from the HTML.

- **BeautifulSoup and Regex Integration:** BeautifulSoup allows you to pass regex patterns to methods like `.find()`, `.find_all()`, and `.select()` to match specific patterns within tag content.
  - ○ **Example: Extracting all email addresses from a webpage:**

    ```python
    Edit
    import requests
    from bs4 import BeautifulSoup
    ```

```python
import re

# Send a GET request to the webpage
response                       =
requests.get('https://example.com')

# Parse the page content with
BeautifulSoup
soup = BeautifulSoup(response.text,
'html.parser')

# Define a regular expression to
match email addresses
email_regex    =    r'[a-zA-Z0-9._%+-
]+@[a-zA-Z0-9.-]+\.[a-zA-Z]{2,}'

# Find all text elements that match
the email regex
emails                         =
soup.find_all(string=re.compile(ema
il_regex))

# Print all found email addresses
for email in emails:
    print(email)
```

- In this example, we use re.compile(email_regex) to compile a regular expression that matches email addresses, and then we search for all instances of that pattern within the text content of the page.

- **Using Regex to Search for Attributes:** You can also use regex to match attributes like `href` (for URLs) or `src` (for images).

  - **Example: Extracting all image URLs from a webpage:**

```python
Edit
img_url_regex = r'https?://[a-zA-Z0-
9./_-]+(?:\.jpg|\.png|\.gif)'

# Find all <img> tags with a src
attribute that matches the regex
images      =      soup.find_all('img',
src=re.compile(img_url_regex))

for img in images:
    print(img['src'])
```

- This regex pattern matches any image URL that ends with `.jpg`, `.png`, or `.gif`.

Practical Example: Extracting Specific Patterns from Scraped Data

Let's look at a more complex example. Imagine you are scraping a product listing page and need to extract all the product prices, which may vary in format (e.g., "$50", "50.00 USD", "€45").

We can use **regex** to extract different price formats from the page.

- **Example: Scraping and Extracting Prices:**

```python
Edit
price_regex                        =
r'\$?\d+(?:,\d{3})*(?:\.\d{2})?\s?(?:USD|
€|GBP)?'

# Find all text elements that match the
price regex
prices                             =
soup.find_all(string=re.compile(price_reg
ex))

# Print all found prices
for price in prices:
    print(price)
```

In this example:

- \d+ matches one or more digits.

155

- `(?:,\d{3})*` allows for commas in larger numbers (e.g., "1,000").
- `(?:\.\d{2})?` matches optional decimal points (e.g., ".99").
- `\s?(?:USD|€|GBP)?` matches optional currency symbols (e.g., "USD", "€").

This regex allows for flexible matching of price formats across different currencies.

Handling Complex Scenarios

Regular expressions become particularly useful when scraping **unclean data**—data that's unstructured, inconsistent, or mixed with extra text. Regex allows you to define rules to extract the precise data you need, even from noisy or unpredictable content.

- **Extracting Mixed Data:** For example, scraping a webpage that lists articles with mixed date formats might require a regex to pull out the dates from inconsistent formats like "12th Jan 2020", "January 12, 2020", or "2020-01-12".
    - **Regex for Extracting Dates:**

      ```python
      python
      Edit
      ```

```
date_regex                          =
r'(\d{1,2}(?:st|nd|rd|th)?\s(?:Jan|
Feb|Mar|Apr|May|Jun|Jul|Aug|Sep|Oct
|Nov|Dec)\s\d{4}|\d{4}-\d{2}-
\d{2})'
dates                               =
soup.find_all(string=re.compile(dat
e_regex))

for date in dates:
    print(date)
```

In this case, the regex matches both date formats "12th Jan 2020" and "2020-01-12" by specifying different date patterns.

Best Practices for Using Regex in Web Scraping

While regex is powerful, it can also be complex and hard to maintain if overused or poorly written. Here are some best practices to keep in mind:

1. **Be Specific:** When writing regular expressions, be as specific as possible to avoid matching unnecessary data. For example, always define the format of the data you expect to extract (e.g., use \d+ for numbers instead of \w+, which matches letters, digits, and underscores).

2. **Test Your Regex:** Use tools like regex101 to test and debug your regular expressions before implementing them in your code.

3. **Avoid Overuse:** While regex is great for extracting patterns, avoid overcomplicating your scraper with regex if the data can be found with simpler methods (like using `.find_all()` with known tag names).

4. **Handle Edge Cases:** Always consider edge cases. If you're scraping dates, for instance, account for different formats, missing data, or non-standard characters.

Conclusion of Chapter 15

In this chapter, we've covered the use of **regular expressions (regex)** in web scraping with BeautifulSoup. Regular expressions are an essential tool for extracting complex and unstructured data from webpages. We've explored:

- The basics of regex syntax and how to use it.
- How to apply regex with BeautifulSoup to extract specific patterns from scraped data.
- Practical examples for extracting data like emails, prices, and dates.
- Best practices for using regex efficiently and correctly.

Regular expressions will greatly enhance your ability to work with messy, unstructured data, enabling you to extract the exact information you need from a webpage. In the next chapter, we'll delve into more advanced techniques, such as scraping large-scale datasets efficiently and optimizing scraping performance.

CHAPTER 16

DATA CLEANING AND PROCESSING

After successfully scraping data from a webpage, you're not always guaranteed that the information you've collected is in a usable format. Raw data often requires cleaning, structuring, and processing before it can be used for analysis. This process is known as **data cleaning**. In this chapter, we'll explore the critical steps involved in cleaning and processing your scraped data using Python, focusing on **Pandas**, a powerful library for data manipulation.

By the end of this chapter, you'll have a good understanding of how to transform your raw, unstructured data into a structured format suitable for analysis.

Cleaning Raw Data for Analysis

Raw data scraped from web pages is rarely perfect. You might encounter issues like:

- **Extra white spaces** in strings

- **Inconsistent formatting** (e.g., different date formats or currency symbols)
- **Missing values** (e.g., empty fields or incomplete data)
- **Malformed or corrupted data** (e.g., incorrect HTML or HTML tags in text fields)
- **Redundant or irrelevant data** (e.g., non-informative text, advertisements, or navigation links)

Cleaning involves identifying and correcting these issues. Here's a high-level overview of the data cleaning process:

1. **Standardize formats:** Ensuring consistency in the format of dates, numbers, and other attributes.
2. **Remove duplicates:** Eliminate redundant data.
3. **Handle missing data:** Identify and deal with any gaps in the data.
4. **Handle errors or outliers:** Correct data that seems out of place or erroneous.

We'll now dive into specific techniques for cleaning data.

Using Pandas to Process Scraped Data

Pandas is one of the most widely used Python libraries for data analysis. It provides powerful tools for working with structured data (such as data frames and series), making it ideal for processing scraped data.

- **Installation**: You can install Pandas with the following:

```bash
Edit
pip install pandas
```

- **DataFrames**: The core data structure in Pandas is the **DataFrame**, which is similar to a table with rows and columns. It's perfect for handling and processing tabular data.
- **Reading Data**: After scraping, you'll often store your data in formats like CSV, JSON, or even databases. Pandas makes it easy to read and process data from these formats.

```python
Edit
import pandas as pd

# Load scraped data from a CSV file
df = pd.read_csv('scraped_data.csv')

# Show the first few rows of the dataframe
print(df.head())
```

Once the data is loaded into a DataFrame, you can begin cleaning it.

Cleaning Techniques in Pandas

- **Removing Extra Whitespaces**: Web data often contains extra spaces, tabs, or newline characters. You can use Pandas to clean these up.

```python
Edit
# Strip whitespace from all column names
df.columns = df.columns.str.strip()

# Remove leading/trailing whitespace from
text columns
df['product_name']                        =
df['product_name'].str.strip()
```

- **Standardizing Data Formats**: Data like dates, prices, and categories can often appear in different formats. It's important to standardize them.
    - **Converting Dates**: If you have dates in different formats, use `pd.to_datetime()` to standardize them into a consistent format.

```python
Edit
df['date']                                =
pd.to_datetime(df['date'],
```

163

```
errors='coerce')  # Coerce errors to
NaT (Not a Time)
```

o **Converting Currency Values**: If your scraped data contains prices in different currencies or formats, you may need to clean and convert them to a common format (e.g., removing currency symbols and commas).

```python
Edit
df['price']                          =
df['price'].replace({'\$': '', ',':
''}, regex=True).astype(float)
```

- **Handling Missing Data**: Missing or incomplete data is a common issue in scraped datasets. Pandas provides several ways to handle missing values:

  o **Identifying Missing Data**: Use `isna()` to detect missing data, and `sum()` to count the number of missing values in each column.

  ```python
  Edit
  print(df.isna().sum())
  ```

  o **Filling Missing Data**: You can fill missing values with a specific value (e.g., a placeholder

string or the column's mean value) using
`fillna()`.

```python
Edit
# Fill missing prices with the column
mean
df['price']                            =
df['price'].fillna(df['price'].mean
())
```

o **Dropping Missing Data**: If a column or row has
too many missing values, you may choose to drop
it altogether.

```python
Edit
# Drop rows with missing prices
df = df.dropna(subset=['price'])
```

- **Handling Duplicates**: Scraped data may include
duplicate entries that need to be removed. You can
remove duplicates based on one or more columns using
`drop_duplicates()`.

```python
Edit
# Remove duplicate rows based on product
names
```

165

```
df                                    =
df.drop_duplicates(subset=['product_name'
])
```

Real-World Example: Cleaning Scraped Product Data for Analysis

Let's walk through an example of cleaning scraped product data from an e-commerce site. The data might include the following columns: product_name, price, category, availability, and rating.

- **Step 1: Load the Data**

```python
Edit
df = pd.read_csv('scraped_products.csv')
```

- **Step 2: Strip Whitespace**

```python
Edit
df.columns = df.columns.str.strip()      #
Strip column names
df['product_name']                       =
df['product_name'].str.strip()     #  Strip
product names
```

- **Step 3: Clean Prices**

The prices might come with dollar signs and commas, so we'll clean them up and convert them to floats.

```python
Edit
df['price']  =  df['price'].replace({'\$':
'', ',': ''}, regex=True).astype(float)
```

- **Step 4: Standardize Availability Data**

If the availability column contains inconsistent values (e.g., "In Stock", "Available", "Out of Stock"), we can standardize these values.

```python
Edit
df['availability']                          =
df['availability'].str.lower().replace({
    'in stock': 'available',
    'out of stock': 'unavailable'
})
```

- **Step 5: Handle Missing Ratings**

If the rating column contains missing values, you could replace them with the mean rating or a placeholder value like "No rating."

```python
```

167

```
Edit
df['rating']   =   df['rating'].fillna('No
rating')
```

- **Step 6: Remove Duplicates**

If you have duplicate product entries, drop them.

```python
Edit
df                                   =
df.drop_duplicates(subset=['product_name'
])
```

- **Step 7: Check for Consistency**

After applying these changes, check for any inconsistencies.

```python
Edit
print(df.head())   # Check the first few
rows to ensure consistency
print(df.isna().sum())   # Check if there
are still missing values
```

Conclusion of Chapter 16

In this chapter, we've covered the essential process of cleaning and processing scraped data using Python's **Pandas** library. Data cleaning is a critical step in web scraping, and it's often where you'll spend most of your time when preparing your scraped data for analysis.

Key takeaways include:

- Using Pandas to load, clean, and process data
- Handling common data issues like missing values, inconsistencies, and formatting issues
- Real-world examples of cleaning product data, including stripping whitespace, handling prices, and removing duplicates

As you continue scraping and working with data, you'll become more adept at identifying and resolving common data issues. In the next chapter, we'll explore how to visualize your cleaned data for insights and analysis.

CHAPTER 17

DATA ANALYSIS WITH PYTHON

Once you've gathered and cleaned your scraped data, the next step is to **analyze** it. This chapter will walk you through using Python's powerful libraries—**Pandas**, **NumPy**, **Matplotlib**, and **Seaborn**—to manipulate and visualize your data. By the end of this chapter, you'll be equipped with the skills to extract meaningful insights from your data and present them in a visually appealing way.

Introduction to Data Analysis in Python

Data analysis refers to the process of inspecting, cleaning, transforming, and modeling data to discover useful information, draw conclusions, and support decision-making. Python has become the go-to language for data analysis because of its simplicity and the robust libraries it offers.

Before you can dive into the analysis, it's essential to understand the structure of your data. You should be comfortable working with **tabular data** (rows and columns) since most web scraping results are stored this way (e.g., product listings, tables of data, etc.).

Key libraries used for data analysis in Python:

- **Pandas**: A versatile library for handling and manipulating structured data (dataframes).
- **NumPy**: A library for numerical operations and array manipulation.
- **Matplotlib**: A plotting library for creating static, animated, and interactive visualizations.
- **Seaborn**: A statistical data visualization library built on top of Matplotlib that provides a high-level interface for drawing attractive and informative graphics.

Using Pandas and NumPy for Data Manipulation

Pandas is the main tool you'll use to manipulate data. It provides the **DataFrame** structure, which is perfect for representing tables of data.

- **Pandas DataFrames**: These are 2-dimensional, size-mutable, and potentially heterogeneous tabular data structures with labeled axes (rows and columns). They make it easy to read and write data, clean and filter data, and perform complex data manipulations.

Here's how to manipulate data using Pandas:

```python
python
```

171

```
Edit
import pandas as pd

# Load data into a DataFrame
df = pd.read_csv('scraped_data.csv')

# Display the first few rows
print(df.head())

# Filtering rows based on a condition
df_filtered = df[df['price'] > 50]    # Get all
products with a price greater than 50

# Sorting data
df_sorted          =          df.sort_values(by='price',
ascending=False)

# Aggregating data
df_aggregated                                          =
df.groupby('category')['price'].mean()                 #
Average price by category
```

NumPy is a library that provides support for large multi-dimensional arrays and matrices, along with a collection of mathematical functions to operate on these arrays.

Example of using NumPy for data analysis:

```
python
Edit
```

```
import numpy as np

# Creating a NumPy array
price_array = np.array(df['price'])

# Finding the mean and standard deviation
mean_price = np.mean(price_array)
std_dev_price = np.std(price_array)

print(f"Mean    Price:    {mean_price},    Standard
Deviation: {std_dev_price}")
```

Visualizing Data with Matplotlib and Seaborn

Once you have cleaned and manipulated your data, the next step is **visualization**. Visualization is a powerful tool that can help reveal patterns, trends, and insights from your data in a clear and effective way.

1. **Matplotlib**: This is the foundational plotting library in Python. It can create a wide range of static, animated, and interactive plots.

Example of a simple line plot using Matplotlib:

```
python
Edit
import matplotlib.pyplot as plt
```

```
# Plotting a simple line chart of prices over
time
plt.plot(df['date'], df['price'])
plt.title('Product Prices Over Time')
plt.xlabel('Date')
plt.ylabel('Price')
plt.show()
```

2. **Seaborn**: Built on top of Matplotlib, Seaborn makes it easier to create attractive and informative statistical graphics. Seaborn provides higher-level functions to generate complex plots with less code.

Example of a scatter plot using Seaborn:

```
python
Edit
import seaborn as sns

# Scatter plot to visualize the relationship
between price and rating
sns.scatterplot(x='price', y='rating', data=df)
plt.title('Price vs. Rating')
plt.show()
```

Seaborn also simplifies the creation of more complex statistical plots, such as **histograms**, **heatmaps**, and **box plots**.

Example of a boxplot to show the distribution of prices across different categories:

```python
Edit
# Boxplot of prices by category
sns.boxplot(x='category', y='price', data=df)
plt.title('Price Distribution by Category')
plt.show()
```

Real-World Example: Analyzing and Visualizing Scraped Data

Let's put everything together in a real-world example. Suppose you scraped product data from an e-commerce site, and the data includes columns such as product_name, price, rating, category, and availability.

- **Step 1: Load the Data**

```python
Edit
import pandas as pd

df = pd.read_csv('scraped_products.csv')
print(df.head())
```

- **Step 2: Data Manipulation**

Let's calculate the average price for each product category:

175

```python
Edit
category_avg_price                              =
df.groupby('category')['price'].mean()
print(category_avg_price)
```

- **Step 3: Visualization**

Next, let's create a bar plot to visualize the average price by category:

```python
Edit
import matplotlib.pyplot as plt
import seaborn as sns

sns.barplot(x=category_avg_price.index,
y=category_avg_price.values)
plt.title('Average Price by Category')
plt.xlabel('Category')
plt.ylabel('Average Price')
plt.xticks(rotation=45)
plt.show()
```

This will display a bar chart showing how prices vary across different product categories.

- **Step 4: Advanced Analysis**

Let's explore the distribution of product ratings:

```python
Edit
sns.histplot(df['rating'], kde=True)
plt.title('Distribution of Product Ratings')
plt.xlabel('Rating')
plt.ylabel('Frequency')
plt.show()
```

- **Step 5: Heatmap of Correlations**

Finally, you might want to visualize correlations between different numerical features (e.g., price and rating):

```python
Edit
correlation_matrix = df[['price', 'rating', 'discount']].corr()
sns.heatmap(correlation_matrix, annot=True, cmap='coolwarm')
plt.title('Correlation Matrix')
plt.show()
```

Conclusion of Chapter 17

In this chapter, we've walked through the essential steps of data analysis in Python. We covered:

- **Pandas and NumPy** for manipulating and analyzing data.

177

- How to **visualize** your data using **Matplotlib** and **Seaborn**.
- Practical examples of analyzing and visualizing scraped product data, including bar plots, histograms, and heatmaps.

By learning how to clean, analyze, and visualize your data, you are now equipped with the necessary skills to derive valuable insights from your web-scraped data. These techniques will be crucial as you continue to work with web scraping projects and strive to turn raw data into actionable information.

CHAPTER 18

SCRAPING AND ANALYZING TEXT DATA

This chapter focuses on extracting and analyzing **text-heavy content**—the kind you often find in product reviews, news articles, blog posts, and social media comments. Unlike structured data (tables, prices, etc.), text requires a different approach. It's messy, nuanced, and full of context. So, scraping it is only half the job—the real challenge lies in making sense of it.

We'll also cover basic **Natural Language Processing (NLP)** tools and how to do **sentiment analysis** using Python libraries. Whether you're trying to analyze customer reviews for a product or gauge public opinion from news headlines, this chapter gives you a practical blueprint.

Scraping Textual Data (Articles, Reviews, etc.)

Before you analyze anything, you need the content. Let's say you want to scrape reviews from an e-commerce website or article text from a news site.

Here's a basic example using `BeautifulSoup` and `requests`:

```python
Edit
import requests
from bs4 import BeautifulSoup

url = 'https://example.com/product-page'
response = requests.get(url)
soup        =        BeautifulSoup(response.text,
'html.parser')

# Extract all review text
reviews = soup.select('.review-text')
texts = [review.get_text(strip=True) for review
in reviews]

for text in texts:
    print(text)
```

If you're dealing with news articles or blog posts, you'd target paragraphs or article tags instead:

```python
Edit
article   =   soup.find('div',   class_='article-
content')
paragraphs = article.find_all('p')
content  =  '  '.join([p.get_text()  for  p  in
paragraphs])
```

Sentiment Analysis on Scraped Text

Once you've scraped the text, the next step is figuring out **what people are saying** and **how they feel about it**. That's where sentiment analysis comes in.

A fast way to get started is using `TextBlob`, which gives you a polarity score for any sentence or document.

Installing TextBlob

```bash
Edit
pip install textblob
python -m textblob.download_corpora
```

Basic Usage

```python
Edit
from textblob import TextBlob

sample_review = "I absolutely love this product! It works like a charm."

blob = TextBlob(sample_review)
print(blob.sentiment)                                    #
Sentiment(polarity=0.75, subjectivity=0.9)
```

181

- **Polarity** ranges from -1 (very negative) to 1 (very positive).
- **Subjectivity** ranges from 0 (objective) to 1 (subjective).

You can run this on a list of reviews:

```python
Edit
for text in texts:
    sentiment = TextBlob(text).sentiment
    print(f"Review:              {text}\nPolarity:
{sentiment.polarity}\n")
```

Using NLP Tools

If you want more control or advanced NLP, move beyond TextBlob. Two of the most widely used libraries for this are:

- **spaCy** – Faster and more scalable.
- **NLTK** – Great for educational purposes and experimentation.

Basic Text Cleaning with NLTK

```python
Edit
import nltk
from nltk.corpus import stopwords
from nltk.tokenize import word_tokenize
```

```
import string

nltk.download('punkt')
nltk.download('stopwords')

text = "This product is amazing. I use it every
day!"

# Tokenize and clean
tokens = word_tokenize(text.lower())
tokens = [word for word in tokens if word not in
stopwords.words('english')   and   word   not   in
string.punctuation]

print(tokens)
```

Real-World Example: Scraping Reviews and Performing Sentiment Analysis

Let's walk through a mini project: scraping product reviews from a sample site and evaluating customer sentiment.

Step 1: Scrape the Reviews

```
python
Edit
url = 'https://fakeshop.com/product/123'
response = requests.get(url)
```

```python
soup          =          BeautifulSoup(response.text,
'html.parser')

review_tags          =          soup.find_all('p',
class_='review')
reviews = [tag.get_text(strip=True)  for  tag  in
review_tags]
```

Step 2: Analyze Sentiment

```python
python
Edit
from textblob import TextBlob

sentiments = []

for review in reviews:
    sentiment                              =
TextBlob(review).sentiment.polarity
    sentiments.append(sentiment)
    print(f"Review: {review} | Sentiment Score:
{sentiment}")
```

Step 3: Visualize Results

```python
python
Edit
import matplotlib.pyplot as plt

plt.hist(sentiments, bins=20, edgecolor='black')
plt.title('Distribution of Sentiment Scores')
plt.xlabel('Sentiment Polarity')
plt.ylabel('Number of Reviews')
```

```
plt.show()
```

This gives you a simple visual representation of how customers feel about a product overall.

Summary of Chapter 18

- You learned how to scrape **textual data** such as articles and reviews.
- We introduced **sentiment analysis** using `TextBlob`, with an optional look at **NLTK** for text processing.
- A full example showed scraping real reviews, calculating sentiment, and visualizing it.

Scraped text is full of insights—but also full of noise. Cleaning it up and analyzing it properly is where the real value lies. In the next chapter, we'll shift gears and look at **building dashboards** to display and interact with your scraped data.

CHAPTER 19

SCRAPING E-COMMERCE SITES

E-commerce websites are goldmines of structured data—product names, prices, ratings, availability, reviews. But they're also built with the clear intent to **deter scraping**. This chapter walks through both **how** to scrape e-commerce data and **how to stay under the radar** while doing it.

Whether you're building a price comparison tool, monitoring competitors, or collecting review trends, you'll need to know how to extract data from heavily guarded and often JavaScript-loaded pages. We'll also walk through a full example scraping and analyzing product data for price comparisons.

Scraping Product Listings, Prices, and Reviews

Let's say you're targeting a generic e-commerce page that looks something like this:

```html
Edit
<div class="product-card">
```

```
<h2      class="product-name">Noise-Cancelling
Headphones</h2>
   <span class="price">$89.99</span>
   <span class="rating">4.5</span>
   <p class="review">Excellent sound quality!</p>
</div>
```

Using BeautifulSoup:

python
Edit
```
import requests
from bs4 import BeautifulSoup

url = 'https://fakeshop.com/search?q=headphones'
headers = {'User-Agent': 'Mozilla/5.0'}
response = requests.get(url, headers=headers)
soup      =      BeautifulSoup(response.text,
'html.parser')

products = soup.find_all('div', class_='product-
card')

for product in products:
    name = product.find('h2', class_='product-
name').text.strip()
    price      =      product.find('span',
class_='price').text.strip()
    rating      =      product.find('span',
class_='rating').text.strip()
```

```
review              =              product.find('p',
class_='review').text.strip()

    print(f'{name}   |   {price}   |   {rating}   |
{review}')
```

Challenges with Scraping E-Commerce Websites

These sites don't want you scraping them. Expect to run into:

- **Bot detection** (Cloudflare, Akamai)
- **Rate-limiting** (Too many requests = temporary ban)
- **JavaScript rendering** (No content in page source)
- **CAPTCHAs**

To bypass these, you'll need to:

- Rotate IPs and User Agents (use `fake_useragent` or proxy services)
- Use headless browsers like **Selenium** for JavaScript-loaded pages
- Set reasonable delays between requests (`time.sleep()` is your friend)
- Pretend to be a human (randomize headers, click patterns if using Selenium)

Working with Structured Data Like Product Ratings

E-commerce sites often present structured data in microformats, schema tags, or JSON-LD scripts. These can save you the trouble of parsing the page manually.

Look for this in the HTML:

```
html
Edit
<script type="application/ld+json">
{
  "@context": "http://schema.org",
  "@type": "Product",
  "name": "Noise-Cancelling Headphones",
  "aggregateRating": {
    "@type": "AggregateRating",
    "ratingValue": "4.5",
    "reviewCount": "234"
  },
  "offers": {
    "price": "89.99",
    "priceCurrency": "USD"
  }
}
</script>
```

You can extract and parse this with:

189

```python
Edit
import json

scripts = soup.find_all('script',
type='application/ld+json')
for script in scripts:
    data = json.loads(script.string)
    if data.get('@type') == 'Product':
        name = data['name']
        price = data['offers']['price']
        rating =
data['aggregateRating']['ratingValue']
        print(f'{name} | ${price} | Rating:
{rating}')
```

Real-World Example: Scraping E-Commerce Data for Price Comparison

Let's say you want to compare headphone prices across two sites.

Step 1: Scrape from Site A

```python
Edit
def scrape_site_a():
    url = 'https://fakeshop-
a.com/products/headphones'
```

```
    soup    =    BeautifulSoup(requests.get(url,
headers=headers).text, 'html.parser')
    results = []
    for item in soup.select('.product-card'):
        name    =    item.select_one('.product-
name').text.strip()
        price                              =
float(item.select_one('.price').text.replace('$
', ''))
        results.append((name, price))
    return results
```

Step 2: Scrape from Site B

```
python
Edit
def scrape_site_b():
    url            =            'https://fakeshop-
b.com/search?q=headphones'
    soup    =    BeautifulSoup(requests.get(url,
headers=headers).text, 'html.parser')
    results = []
    for item in soup.select('.item'):
        name                               =
item.select_one('.title').text.strip()
        price                              =
float(item.select_one('.amount').text.replace('
$', ''))
        results.append((name, price))
    return results
```

191

Step 3: Compare and Print Differences

```python
Edit
a_data = scrape_site_a()
b_data = scrape_site_b()

comparison = {}

for name, price in a_data + b_data:
    if name not in comparison:
        comparison[name] = []
    comparison[name].append(price)

for product, prices in comparison.items():
    if len(prices) > 1:
        print(f"{product} - Site A: ${prices[0]} | Site B: ${prices[1]} | Diff: ${abs(prices[0] - prices[1]):.2f}")
```

Summary of Chapter 19

- We broke down how to extract product names, prices, and reviews.

- You saw real issues like bot detection, JavaScript rendering, and how to work around them.

- You learned how to extract structured data and parse JSON-LD blocks.

- We built a working script for cross-site price comparison.

E-commerce scraping isn't plug-and-play. It takes patience, some sneakiness, and a good understanding of how websites are built. In the next chapter, we'll focus on **scaling your scraping operation**—making it faster, smarter, and more resilient.

CHAPTER 20

SCRAPING NEWS AND SOCIAL MEDIA

Scraping news sites and social media platforms is where things start to feel like walking through a minefield. On one hand, you're dealing with massive sources of real-time information. On the other hand, you're bumping up against platforms that **actively block scraping** and often have **strict terms of service**. This chapter walks the line carefully, showing you how to get what you need *without* tripping any alarms.

Scraping News Sites for Headlines and Articles

Most traditional news sites are still HTML-based and relatively scrape-friendly—if you're respectful.

Example: Scraping Headlines from a News Site

Let's take a hypothetical page layout:

```
html
Edit
<article class="news-article">
```

194

```
<h2    class="headline">New    AI    Breakthrough
Announced</h2>
    <p class="summary">Researchers unveiled...</p>
</article>
```

Using BeautifulSoup:

```python
Edit
import requests
from bs4 import BeautifulSoup

url = 'https://fakenews.com/tech'
headers = {'User-Agent': 'Mozilla/5.0'}
response = requests.get(url, headers=headers)
soup        =        BeautifulSoup(response.text,
'html.parser')

articles        =        soup.find_all('article',
class_='news-article')

for article in articles:
    headline        =        article.find('h2',
class_='headline').text.strip()
    summary        =        article.find('p',
class_='summary').text.strip()
    print(f'{headline} - {summary}')
```

Quick tip: Don't scrape hundreds of pages in a row. Be nice. Timeouts and polite headers go a long way.

Scraping Social Media Data (Twitter, Instagram, etc.)

Let's not sugarcoat it: scraping social media is hard. Platforms like **Twitter**, **Instagram**, and **Facebook** are extremely aggressive about blocking non-API traffic. You have three main options:

1. Use the API (if available)

This is the cleanest route.

Example: Twitter API via Tweepy
python
Edit
```python
import tweepy

client = tweepy.Client(bearer_token='YOUR_BEARER_TOKEN')
response = client.get_recent_tweets_with_hashtag("#ai", max_results=10)

for tweet in response.data:
    print(tweet.text)
```

Downsides? Rate limits. Also, APIs tend to give *only* what they want you to see.

2. Headless Browsers (Selenium)

When APIs fall short or you want full page content.

```python
Edit
from selenium import webdriver
from bs4 import BeautifulSoup

driver = webdriver.Chrome()
driver.get("https://twitter.com/search?q=%23AI&
src=typed_query")

soup      =       BeautifulSoup(driver.page_source,
'html.parser')
tweets = soup.find_all('div',  attrs={'data-
testid': 'tweet'})

for tweet in tweets[:5]:
    print(tweet.get_text(strip=True))

driver.quit()
```

Caveat: Twitter and Instagram rotate class names and layouts *constantly*—you'll be in maintenance hell.

3. Third-Party Scraper APIs (ScraperAPI, Apify, etc.)

These take care of proxying, rendering, and anti-bot for you. But you're trusting them with your data and usage.

Understanding the Ethical Implications of Scraping Social Media

This part matters. Here's the hard truth: **just because you can scrape something doesn't mean you should**.

- Most social platforms have **explicit terms prohibiting scraping.**
- You're potentially pulling data from **private users** who didn't consent.
- Some jurisdictions (hello, GDPR) have **legal penalties** for scraping PII or using scraped data inappropriately.

Ask yourself:

- Is this data publicly available without login?
- Are you storing or republishing someone else's content?
- Could the data identify someone personally?

If the answer is yes to any of those—either get proper access or find another way.

Real-World Example: Scraping Twitter for Trending Hashtags

Let's use `snscrape`, a Python library that doesn't use the official API but still works under the hood through Twitter's public frontend.

Install:

```bash
Edit
pip install snscrape
```

Use:

```python
Edit
import snscrape.modules.twitter as sntwitter

query = "from:verge since:2023-01-01 until:2023-01-31"
tweets = []

for i, tweet in enumerate(sntwitter.TwitterSearchScraper(query).get_items()):
    if i > 10:
        break
    tweets.append(tweet.content)
```

```
for t in tweets:
    print(t)
```

You can tweak the query to pull hashtags, users, dates, etc.

Summary of Chapter 20

- News sites are easier to scrape than social media—use headers and delays.
- For social platforms, the API is your best bet. If you go headless, be ready for breakage.
- Ethical scraping is more than a checkbox—don't ignore legal gray zones.
- Tools like `snscrape` can give you structured social media data with less pain than Selenium.

Next up: **scaling your scrapers with multithreading and queues** to speed things up without burning your IP.

CHAPTER 21

CREATING A WEB SCRAPING PROJECT

Now that you have a solid understanding of web scraping techniques, it's time to get hands-on and **create a complete web scraping project** from scratch. In this chapter, we'll guide you through the process of **planning, structuring**, and **executing** a scraping project. We'll also touch on important concepts like **dependency management, version control** with Git, and how to make your scraper efficient and maintainable.

Defining the Scope of a Scraping Project

Before you write a single line of code, **define the scope** of your project. This will help you stay focused, determine the complexity, and prevent you from collecting unnecessary data.

Key Questions to Ask Yourself:

- **What is the goal?**
  Are you collecting product data for price comparison?

Scraping job listings for analysis? Or gathering news headlines for sentiment analysis?

- **Which data do you need?** Identify exactly what data you want to scrape. For example, for product data, you might need: product name, price, reviews, and product description.

- **How frequently will you scrape?** Are you scraping data once or periodically? The frequency will affect how you handle rate limits, pagination, and storage.

- **What are the legal and ethical boundaries?** As you get more specific with your scope, ensure that you're following the website's terms of service. Be mindful of **robots.txt** and any anti-scraping measures.

Planning and Structuring a Web Scraper

Once you've defined the scope, it's time to plan how you will build your scraper. Think about how you will structure your project and break it down into smaller, manageable tasks.

1. Break the Project into Modules

A scraper typically has different components like:

- **Data extraction**: The part that pulls the raw data from web pages.
- **Data cleaning**: Processes that clean the raw data and get it into a structured format.
- **Storage**: Saving the data (CSV, database, etc.).
- **Logging**: Keeping track of the scraper's progress and errors.

For instance, your folder structure might look like this:

```
kotlin
Edit
web_scraping_project/
|
├── scraper/
|    ├── __init__.py
|    ├── extract_data.py
|    ├── clean_data.py
|    ├── store_data.py
|    └── log.py
|
├── data/
|    └── scraped_data.csv
|
├── requirements.txt
└── README.md
```

2. Use Functions and Classes

When designing your scraper, organize your code into **functions** and **classes** to make it modular and reusable. For example:

- A function to **fetch HTML content** using the `requests` library.
- A function to **parse and extract data** using `BeautifulSoup`.
- A class for **logging** progress, errors, and success messages.

Example Code Snippet:

```python
Edit
import requests
from bs4 import BeautifulSoup

def fetch_html(url):
    """Fetch HTML content of a page."""
    headers = {'User-Agent': 'Mozilla/5.0'}
    response = requests.get(url, headers=headers)
    if response.status_code == 200:
        return response.text
    else:
        print(f"Failed to retrieve {url}")
        return None
```

```python
def extract_data(soup):
    """Extract specific data using
BeautifulSoup."""
    titles = soup.find_all('h2',
class_='product-title')
    prices = soup.find_all('span',
class_='price')

    data = []
    for title, price in zip(titles, prices):
        data.append({
            'title': title.text.strip(),
            'price': price.text.strip()
        })
    return data
```

Managing Dependencies and Version Control (Git)

A crucial step in any project is **managing dependencies** and **keeping track of code changes** using version control. This makes it easier to maintain the project, collaborate with others, and track what has changed.

1. Setting Up Virtual Environments

To avoid conflicts with other Python projects, it's good practice to create a **virtual environment** for your scraping project. This isolates dependencies and ensures that they're project-specific.

```bash
Edit
# Create a virtual environment
python3 -m venv venv

# Activate the virtual environment (Linux/macOS)
source venv/bin/activate

# Activate the virtual environment (Windows)
venv\Scripts\activate
```

2. Install Dependencies

Once your environment is active, install the libraries you'll need (e.g., requests, beautifulsoup4, pandas, etc.).

```bash
Edit
pip install requests beautifulsoup4 pandas
```

3. Create a requirements.txt File

To make your project easily reproducible, generate a requirements.txt file. This will list all the libraries and their versions required to run your project.

```bash
Edit
pip freeze > requirements.txt
```

Now, anyone who clones your project can install the necessary dependencies with:

```bash
Edit
pip install -r requirements.txt
```

4. Initialize a Git Repository

Git is an essential tool for version control. Initialize a Git repository to keep track of your code changes, commits, and collaboration.

```bash
Edit
# Initialize Git repository
git init

# Add all files to Git
git add .

# Commit changes
git commit -m "Initial commit for web scraping project"
```

5. Pushing to GitHub

If you want to share your project or collaborate with others, create a repository on GitHub and push your local repository to GitHub.

```
bash
Edit
git        remote        add        origin
https://github.com/yourusername/your-repo.git
git push -u origin master
```

Real-World Example: Building a Web Scraper for a Specific Data Source

Let's say you want to build a scraper that collects product data from an e-commerce site. Here's how you could break it down:

Step 1: Define the Target URL and Data

- You want to scrape product names, prices, and descriptions from a site like "FakeShop."

Step 2: Build the Scraper

1. **Send a Request** to the product page.
2. **Parse the HTML** with BeautifulSoup.
3. **Extract the data** (names, prices, etc.).

4. **Store the data** in a CSV file.

```python
Edit
import csv
import requests
from bs4 import BeautifulSoup

def fetch_data(url):
    """Fetch data from the product page."""
    response = requests.get(url)
    soup = BeautifulSoup(response.text,
'html.parser')
    return extract_product_data(soup)

def extract_product_data(soup):
    """Extract product names, prices, and
descriptions."""
    products = []
    for product in soup.select('.product-card'):
        name = product.find('h3',
class_='product-name').text.strip()
        price = product.find('span',
class_='price').text.strip()
        description = product.find('p',
class_='product-description').text.strip()
        products.append([name, price,
description])
    return products
```

```
def save_to_csv(data, filename="products.csv"):
    """Save the extracted data to a CSV file."""
    with open(filename, mode='w', newline='') as
file:
        writer = csv.writer(file)
        writer.writerow(['Name',          'Price',
'Description'])
        writer.writerows(data)


# Main script
url = 'https://fakeshop.com/products'
data = fetch_data(url)
save_to_csv(data)
```

Step 3: Run the Scraper

Run your scraper and verify that the data is being extracted correctly and saved to a CSV file.

Summary of Chapter 21

- **Defining the scope** of your project will help you focus on the data you need and avoid unnecessary complexity.
- **Structuring your scraper** involves creating a modular design, using functions and classes to keep everything organized.

- **Managing dependencies** through virtual environments and **version control with Git** ensures that your project stays maintainable and collaborative.
- We built a **real-world scraper** from scratch, pulling product data and saving it in a CSV file.

In the next chapter, we will discuss how to **scale your scraping project** using techniques like multithreading, job queues, and distributed systems to handle large volumes of data.

CHAPTER 22

MANAGING AND SCALING SCRAPING PROJECTS

As your scraping projects grow in complexity and size, managing and scaling them effectively becomes essential. Whether you're dealing with **massive datasets**, **real-time data collection**, or **scraping across many websites**, this chapter will guide you through the key strategies for **scaling** your projects to meet these demands.

In this chapter, we'll explore techniques like **multithreading**, **multiprocessing**, and **distributed scraping** to handle large-scale scraping tasks efficiently. We'll also look at **error handling** and managing **data flow** in more advanced scraping projects.

Scaling Scraping Projects to Handle Large Datasets

As you scrape data from multiple pages or sources, the volume of data quickly increases, and the script's performance may begin to slow down. Scaling your scraping operations ensures that the script runs efficiently even when dealing with massive amounts of data.

Key Strategies for Scaling:

1. **Pagination Handling**: As we covered in earlier chapters, scraping multiple pages through **pagination** is one of the most common methods to collect large datasets. To scale, make sure that your scraper can handle large numbers of pages without timeouts or data loss.

2. **Batch Processing**: Instead of scraping all data in one go, split it into smaller **batches** that can be processed sequentially or in parallel. This helps to avoid overwhelming your system with memory overload and increases reliability.

3. **Database Optimization**: Storing large datasets in **SQL** or **NoSQL databases** (e.g., MySQL, MongoDB) is far more efficient than writing to CSV or JSON files. This also facilitates **querying and analysis** of the data.

4. **Data Deduplication**: When scraping across multiple sources or pages, ensure you have methods to handle duplicates in the collected data. This can be done through **checksums** or **hashing** to identify and discard duplicate entries.

Using Multithreading and Multiprocessing for Parallel Scraping

When you're scraping large numbers of pages or performing multiple independent tasks (like scraping from different websites), **parallelizing** your code can significantly speed up the process. Two common approaches to parallel scraping are **multithreading** and **multiprocessing**.

Multithreading for Scraping

Multithreading allows multiple tasks to run concurrently within a single process. It's ideal when you need to perform many I/O-bound operations, like fetching data from websites. Python's `threading` **module** provides a simple way to handle multiple threads in one program.

Advantages of Multithreading:

- Efficient for I/O-bound tasks, such as making HTTP requests.
- Allows you to scrape data concurrently without needing multiple processes.

Example:

```python
Edit
```

```python
import threading
import requests
from bs4 import BeautifulSoup

# Function to fetch and parse data
def fetch_and_parse(url):
    response = requests.get(url)
    soup      =      BeautifulSoup(response.text,
'html.parser')
    # Extract data here
    print(f"Data from {url} extracted.")

# List of URLs to scrape
urls      =      ['https://example.com/page1',
'https://example.com/page2',
'https://example.com/page3']

# Create threads for each URL
threads = []
for url in urls:
    thread                                    =
threading.Thread(target=fetch_and_parse,
args=(url,))
    threads.append(thread)
    thread.start()

# Wait for all threads to complete
for thread in threads:
    thread.join()
```

```
print("Scraping completed.")
```

Multiprocessing for Scraping

For CPU-bound tasks (like data processing or intensive computations), **multiprocessing** can be a better option. The **multiprocessing module** allows you to create separate processes that run concurrently, taking full advantage of multiple CPU cores.

Advantages of Multiprocessing:

- Best for CPU-bound tasks.
- Uses separate memory spaces, reducing issues with thread contention.

Example:

```python
Edit
import multiprocessing
import requests
from bs4 import BeautifulSoup

# Function to fetch and parse data
def fetch_and_parse(url):
    response = requests.get(url)
    soup     =        BeautifulSoup(response.text,
'html.parser')
```

```
    # Extract data here
    print(f"Data from {url} extracted.")

# List of URLs to scrape
urls        =        ['https://example.com/page1',
'https://example.com/page2',
'https://example.com/page3']

# Create a pool of processes
with multiprocessing.Pool(processes=3) as pool:
    pool.map(fetch_and_parse, urls)

print("Scraping completed.")
```

Managing Data Flow and Error Handling in Large Projects

When scaling up your web scraping projects, error handling becomes even more crucial. A large-scale scraping operation can encounter various issues like **timeouts, HTTP errors, IP blocking**, or **data inconsistencies**.

Best Practices for Error Handling:

1. **Retry Logic**: Implement **retry mechanisms** to handle temporary issues like timeouts or HTTP 500 errors. For

example, you can use the **requests library's `Retry`** **feature** or a custom retry strategy with `time.sleep()`.

2. **Timeouts and Delays**: Always set **timeouts** for HTTP requests to avoid hanging indefinitely when a page takes too long to load. Introduce **delays** or **randomize delays** between requests to avoid being detected as a bot.

3. **Logging Errors**: Log all errors with appropriate details, such as the URL, error type, and the specific part of the code that failed. This will help you troubleshoot and identify patterns in failures.

4. **Handling Captchas and Anti-Scraping Mechanisms**: Scraping sites with aggressive anti-scraping measures requires additional error handling. For example, you might need to rotate **IP addresses** using proxies, simulate human browsing behavior (e.g., using **Selenium** or **Pyppeteer**), or use services like **2Captcha** to solve CAPTCHAs.

Real-World Example: Scaling a Scraping Script for Real-Time Data Collection

Let's say you need to collect **real-time stock data** from multiple finance websites. These sites update their information frequently, and you need to scrape large amounts of data efficiently.

Here's how you can scale this scraping project:

1. **Use Multithreading or Multiprocessing**: Use multithreading to scrape data from multiple sites simultaneously, or multiprocessing to handle intensive processing tasks (such as analyzing the data in real time).

2. **Periodic Scraping**: Use **Task Scheduler** (on Windows) or **Cron jobs** (on Linux) to run the scraping script at regular intervals, like every minute or every hour.

3. **Real-time Data Storage**: Instead of saving to a CSV file, you might save the data directly into a **database** (e.g., MySQL or PostgreSQL) to ensure data consistency and real-time querying.

4. **Error Handling for Real-Time Scraping**: Set up **timeouts, retries**, and logging to make sure that if a website goes down temporarily, your script can recover without data loss.

5. **Scaling with Cloud**: If the dataset grows beyond what your local system can handle, consider deploying your scraper on the cloud (e.g., AWS EC2 or Google Cloud) and utilizing distributed processing frameworks like **Apache Spark** for scraping and processing data at scale.

Example Code Snippet for Real-Time Scraping:

```
python
Edit
import requests
```

```python
from bs4 import BeautifulSoup
import time
from threading import Thread

# Function to scrape stock data from a website
def scrape_stock_data(url):
    response = requests.get(url)
    soup      =      BeautifulSoup(response.text,
'html.parser')
    # Process the data here
    print(f"Real-time data scraped from {url}")

# List of URLs to scrape
urls     =     ['https://finance.com/stock1',
'https://finance.com/stock2',
'https://finance.com/stock3']

# Function to run the scraping periodically
def run_scraper_periodically():
    while True:
        threads = []
        for url in urls:
            thread                              =
Thread(target=scrape_stock_data, args=(url,))
            threads.append(thread)
            thread.start()

        # Wait for all threads to finish
        for thread in threads:
```

```
        thread.join()

        # Sleep before the next scraping
        time.sleep(60)   # Scrape every minute

# Start the periodic scraping
run_scraper_periodically()
```

Summary of Chapter 22

In this chapter, we explored key strategies for managing and scaling web scraping projects:

- **Scaling** your scraper to handle large datasets requires efficient handling of data extraction, storage, and pagination.
- **Multithreading** and **multiprocessing** can speed up scraping by allowing parallel data collection or processing.
- **Error handling** is critical in large-scale projects, where you'll face timeouts, anti-scraping measures, and data inconsistencies.
- We discussed a **real-world example** of scaling a scraping script for real-time stock data collection.

221

In the next chapter, we'll take a deep dive into **data analysis and visualization**, using tools like Pandas, Matplotlib, and Seaborn to turn your scraped data into actionable insights.

CHAPTER 23

WEB SCRAPING FOR SEO AND COMPETITIVE ANALYSIS

In this chapter, we will explore how web scraping can be used to gain valuable insights into SEO (Search Engine Optimization) and perform competitive analysis. Whether you're optimizing your website or analyzing your competitors' strategies, web scraping allows you to collect key SEO metrics from the web, identify trends, and make data-driven decisions.

We'll break down the process of scraping data for SEO, covering important elements like **meta tags**, **backlinks**, and other SEO-related components. Additionally, we'll dive into how web scraping can be leveraged for **competitive analysis** to help you understand what your competitors are doing right (or wrong), and how you can use that information to enhance your own SEO strategies.

Scraping for SEO

Search Engine Optimization (SEO) is an ongoing process that requires continuous monitoring and analysis. Web scraping can help you collect critical data points that contribute to your website's SEO performance and improve its ranking on search engines.

Key SEO Elements to Scrape:

1. **Meta Tags**: These include meta descriptions, titles, and keywords that are used by search engines to index content. Scraping this data across multiple websites can help you understand how your competitors optimize their content and identify opportunities for improvement.
   - **Meta Title**: The title tag that appears in search results and browser tabs.
   - **Meta Description**: A brief description of the content, which appears under the title in search results.
   - **Meta Keywords**: A list of keywords the page is targeting.

   Example:

```python
Edit
import requests
from bs4 import BeautifulSoup

def scrape_meta_tags(url):
    response = requests.get(url)
```

```
soup    =    BeautifulSoup(response.text,
'html.parser')
    title = soup.find('title').text
    description    =    soup.find('meta',
attrs={'name': 'description'})
    keywords    =    soup.find('meta',
attrs={'name': 'keywords'})

    meta_description    =
description['content'] if description else
'No description'
    meta_keywords = keywords['content'] if
keywords else 'No keywords'

    print(f"Title: {title}")
    print(f"Description:
{meta_description}")
    print(f"Keywords: {meta_keywords}")

scrape_meta_tags('https://example.com')
```

2. **Backlinks**: Backlinks are one of the most important ranking factors in SEO. Scraping data on backlinks allows you to track the websites linking to your competitors and identify potential backlink opportunities.

   o **Anchor Text**: The clickable text in a hyperlink that links back to a page.

   o **Backlink Quantity**: The number of backlinks pointing to a page.

225

o **Referring Domains**: Unique websites that are linking back to a given page.

Tools like **Ahrefs, Moz,** and **SEMrush** provide backlink data, but scraping these backlinks using Python can give you a custom view of competitors' link profiles, if available.

3. **Headings and Content**: Scraping headings (H1, H2, etc.) on competitor sites can reveal their content structure, keywords, and topics. Analyzing this will help you improve your own content structure for SEO purposes.

o **H1**: Main heading tag, generally used for the page's title.

o **H2, H3, etc.**: Subheadings used to structure the content.

Example:

```python
Edit
def scrape_headings(url):
    response = requests.get(url)
    soup = BeautifulSoup(response.text,
'html.parser')
    headings = soup.find_all(['h1', 'h2',
'h3'])
```

```
for heading in headings:
    print(f"{heading.name}:
{heading.text.strip()}")


scrape_headings('https://example.com')
```

4. **Page Speed and Performance Data**: SEO isn't only about content. Page speed is a ranking factor for search engines like Google. Tools like **Google PageSpeed Insights** can help you scrape performance data, such as load time, and render-blocking resources, giving you actionable insights on how to optimize your site for faster loading.

5. **Images and Alt Text**: Images can also contribute to SEO when properly optimized with descriptive **alt text**. Scraping image data and checking if **alt attributes** are used properly can give you valuable insights.

Competitive Analysis through Web Scraping

Competitive analysis is critical in SEO, as it helps you understand how your competitors are optimizing their websites and where you can improve. Web scraping offers a powerful way to track your competitors' rankings, keywords, backlinks, content strategies, and overall site structure.

Key Aspects to Scrape for Competitive Analysis:

1. **Keyword Analysis**: Scraping competitors' content to identify the keywords they're targeting can help you fine-tune your own SEO strategy. By analyzing the frequency and placement of keywords in titles, headers, and body content, you can discover the key terms and phrases that are driving traffic to their site.

2. **Site Structure and URL Patterns**: Analyzing how your competitors structure their websites, including URL patterns, can provide you with a roadmap to organize your own site's pages for better SEO performance.

   o **URL structure**: Clean, well-organized URLs with relevant keywords contribute to better SEO.

   o **Internal linking**: Scraping the internal link structure can help you identify how competitors guide users and search engines across their site.

3. **Content Quality and Length**: Scraping the length and quality of your competitors' content can help you assess the kind of content that is ranking well for your target keywords. If your competitors are ranking highly for certain terms, their content may be longer or more in-depth, or they may have better formatting, such as images or videos.

4. **Competitor Backlink Profiles**: Knowing where your competitors' backlinks are coming from allows you to pursue similar opportunities. Scraping backlink data from

competitor websites (using APIs from backlink tools or directly from the site's source code) can uncover strategic link-building opportunities.

Tools and Techniques for SEO Scraping

While BeautifulSoup and Requests are great tools for scraping data, certain SEO-related data may require specialized tools or libraries to scrape effectively. Here are some recommended tools:

1. **BeautifulSoup & Requests**: Great for scraping general SEO data, such as meta tags, headings, and page content.

2. **Scrapy**: An advanced web scraping framework that supports complex, large-scale scrapes. Scrapy is more efficient for scraping large volumes of data and is ideal for SEO analysis when you're scraping multiple pages or entire websites.

3. **Selenium**: When scraping dynamic content that relies on JavaScript (like Google Search Results or social media posts), **Selenium** can render JavaScript and interact with pages just like a user would.

4. **LXML**: A faster, more efficient alternative to BeautifulSoup, especially for large-scale scraping projects where performance is a concern.

5. **Google Search API**: For scraping search engine results and analyzing competitors' rankings. You can extract the ranking positions, titles, and snippets from search engine result pages (SERPs).

Real-World Example: Analyzing Competitor Websites for SEO Insights

Let's consider you're trying to perform an SEO analysis on a competitor's e-commerce site. You'll want to scrape and analyze the following:

- **Meta Tags**: Extract meta titles, descriptions, and keywords to evaluate how well they are optimized.
- **Backlinks**: Gather data about where the competitor's backlinks are coming from, helping you build your own link-building strategy.
- **Content**: Scrape product descriptions, titles, and reviews to identify which keywords they are targeting.

Example:

```python
Edit
def analyze_competitor_seo(url):
    # Scraping meta tags for SEO
```

```python
    response = requests.get(url)
    soup        =        BeautifulSoup(response.text,
'html.parser')
    title = soup.find('title').text
    meta_description      =      soup.find('meta',
attrs={'name': 'description'})['content']
    meta_keywords       =       soup.find('meta',
attrs={'name': 'keywords'})['content']

    print(f"Competitor Meta Title: {title}")
    print(f"Competitor    Meta    Description:
{meta_description}")
    print(f"Competitor     Meta     Keywords:
{meta_keywords}")

    # Scraping headings to analyze content
structure
    headings = soup.find_all(['h1', 'h2', 'h3'])
    for heading in headings:
        print(f"Heading:     {heading.name}    -
{heading.text.strip()}")

analyze_competitor_seo('https://competitor.com'
)
```

Summary of Chapter 23

In this chapter, we explored how **web scraping** can be used to gather valuable SEO insights and perform **competitive analysis**. We discussed how to scrape important SEO data, such as **meta tags**, **backlinks**, **headings**, and **images**, and how these elements can be used to refine your own SEO strategies. Additionally, we covered tools like **BeautifulSoup**, **Scrapy**, and **Selenium**, and provided a real-world example of analyzing a competitor's website for SEO insights.

In the next chapter, we will discuss **ethical considerations** in web scraping, focusing on best practices to ensure your scraping activities are legal, ethical, and compliant with website terms of service.

CHAPTER 24

LEGAL AND ETHICAL ASPECTS OF WEB SCRAPING

While web scraping is a powerful tool for gathering data from the web, it comes with **legal** and **ethical considerations** that must be carefully navigated. Failing to understand the risks and responsibilities associated with scraping can lead to **legal consequences** and damage to your reputation. This chapter will explore the **legal risks** of web scraping, the importance of respecting **robots.txt** files, and the best practices for ensuring that your web scraping activities remain ethical and compliant with the law.

Legal Risks of Web Scraping (TOS, right Issues)

Web scraping can pose several legal risks, particularly when it comes to **violating terms of service (TOS)** agreements and **right** protections. It's essential to be aware of these potential issues before scraping any website.

1. Violating Terms of Service (TOS)

Most websites have a **Terms of Service** agreement that governs how users can interact with the site. Many of these terms explicitly forbid the use of scraping tools to collect data. Violating these terms can result in **legal action**, including lawsuits, fines, or being permanently banned from accessing the site.

For example:

- **Case Study**: In 2017, **LinkedIn** filed a lawsuit against **hiQ Labs**, a data analytics company, for scraping user profiles without permission. While the court ruled in favor of **hiQ Labs**, the case highlighted the potential risks of scraping a site against its TOS.

Key Takeaway: Always read and understand the **TOS** of any website you intend to scrape. If scraping is prohibited, seek permission or consider alternative approaches, like using an **API** if one is provided.

2. right and Intellectual Property Issues

In some cases, the content you scrape from a website may be righted. This is particularly relevant when scraping **media**, such as **images**, **videos**, **articles**, or **product descriptions**.

234

- **Case Study**: A 2016 case between **Oracle** and **Google** discussed whether scraping could violate rights. While this case was about Google's use of Java code, it exemplifies the broader concern over **intellectual property** in scraped content.

Key Takeaway: If you're scraping content that could be protected by right (e.g., articles, images), ensure you are not violating intellectual property rights. Avoid directly ing and republishing such content unless you have permission or it falls under **fair use**.

3. Data Protection and Privacy Laws

In some jurisdictions, scraping personal data can violate data protection laws like **GDPR** (General Data Protection Regulation) in the EU or **CCPA** (California Consumer Privacy Act) in the U.S. Scraping personal information without consent, such as email addresses or user profiles, can result in severe penalties.

Key Takeaway: Be mindful of **data privacy** laws when scraping personal data. Always ensure that you're complying with relevant regulations, especially when handling sensitive information.

Respecting robots.txt Files

The **robots.txt** file is a **standard** used by websites to guide the behavior of web crawlers and scraping tools. This file tells crawlers which pages on a website should not be scraped or indexed by search engines. It's important to respect the instructions set by the robots.txt file to ensure your scraping activities are ethical.

What is robots.txt?

A **robots.txt** file is a simple text file located at the root of a website that tells search engine bots and scrapers which pages they are allowed or not allowed to access. For example, a robots.txt file might contain instructions like:

```
makefile
Edit
User-agent: *
Disallow: /private/
Disallow: /login/
```

In this example:

- **User-agent**: * refers to all bots (or scrapers).
- **Disallow**: /private/ and /login/ indicate that these pages should not be accessed by web crawlers.

Should You Always Respect robots.txt?

While robots.txt is widely accepted as a guideline for ethical scraping, it is **not legally binding** in all cases. Some websites may block certain crawlers using robots.txt to prevent overload or protect content, but it does not necessarily mean scraping is illegal. However, adhering to the robots.txt guidelines is considered best practice and demonstrates that you respect the website's rules.

Key Takeaway: Always check and respect the **robots.txt** file of any website you intend to scrape. If scraping is disallowed on certain pages, avoid scraping those parts of the site. If in doubt, contact the website owner for clarification or permission.

Best Practices for Ethical Web Scraping

To ensure your web scraping activities are ethical, you should follow several best practices. These practices not only help you avoid legal issues but also minimize the strain your scraping has on websites and servers.

1. Respect Website Traffic and Load

One of the primary ethical considerations when scraping is **server load**. Scraping too aggressively or scraping too frequently can place unnecessary load on a website's servers, causing delays or outages.

Best Practices for Traffic and Load Management:

- **Limit request frequency**: Use **delays** between requests to prevent overloading the server. For example, add a random delay between each request using `time.sleep()` in Python.
- **Use a User-Agent string**: Set a custom **User-Agent** string that identifies your scraper, so webmasters can know who is scraping their site.
- **Avoid scraping during peak hours**: If possible, schedule your scraping tasks during low-traffic periods to avoid disrupting website performance.

2. Use Official APIs Whenever Possible

Many websites offer **APIs** that provide structured and legal access to their data. Whenever available, use these APIs instead of scraping the website directly. APIs are designed to allow data access in a controlled and regulated manner, ensuring compliance with the site's TOS.

Key Takeaway: If a website offers an API, use it. Scraping should be a last resort when no API is available, or when the API doesn't offer the data you need.

3. Avoid Scraping Personal or Sensitive Data

If you're scraping public data, always be cautious about scraping personal or sensitive information. Data protection laws such as **GDPR** (EU) and **CCPA** (California) impose strict rules on how personal data should be collected, processed, and stored.

Best Practices for Handling Sensitive Data:

- **Anonymize data**: If scraping data with personal information, anonymize it to ensure privacy.
- **Obtain consent**: If necessary, get explicit consent from the data subject before scraping their personal data.

4. Be Transparent About Your Scraping Activities

Whenever possible, reach out to website owners or administrators to **request permission** before scraping their content. Being transparent shows that you respect their rights and are operating in good faith.

- **Notify website owners**: Send a request to the site owner or administrator if you're scraping a site that could be sensitive or has strict TOS guidelines.
- **Provide your contact details**: When scraping data, it's good practice to include a contact email or URL in the headers of your requests so the website owner can reach you if necessary.

Real-World Example: Navigating Legal Boundaries in Scraping

Let's consider a scenario where you want to scrape **job listings** from a popular job search website for a data analysis project. You check the site's robots.txt file and notice it prohibits scraping on certain pages, including the listings page.

Here's how you can navigate the legal boundaries:

1. **Check the Terms of Service**: You read through the TOS of the website and see that scraping job listings is prohibited. This presents a legal risk if you proceed.

2. **Use an API (if available)**: The website offers an **API** that provides job listing data in a structured format. You decide to use the API instead of scraping the website directly.

3. **Contact the Website Owner**: If the API doesn't cover all the data you need, you reach out to the website owner, explaining your purpose and asking for permission to scrape the data.

4. **Scraping with Ethics**: If the owner approves, you proceed to scrape, ensuring that you respect the **rate limits** and avoid overloading their servers by adding delays between requests.

240

Key Takeaway: Navigating the legal and ethical aspects of web scraping requires being proactive about understanding **TOS**, checking for an **API**, and respecting the **robots.txt** file. Always make sure your scraping activities are transparent, respectful, and compliant with legal requirements.

Summary of Chapter 24

In this chapter, we examined the **legal** and **ethical** aspects of web scraping, including the risks associated with violating **terms of service**, **right**, and **data protection laws**. We discussed the importance of respecting **robots.txt** files and following best practices for ethical scraping, such as limiting request frequency and using official APIs. We also explored a **real-world example** of navigating legal boundaries when scraping job listing data.

In the next chapter, we will explore **advanced scraping techniques**, including how to handle dynamic websites, use headless browsers, and manage CAPTCHAs.

CHAPTER 25

KEEPING YOUR SCRAPER EFFICIENT AND FAST

Performance matters — especially when your scraper needs to handle large volumes of data, run on a schedule, or stay under the radar. A slow or sloppy scraper isn't just inefficient — it's more likely to get blocked, burn unnecessary resources, and annoy the websites you're targeting. This chapter is all about **scraping smart**: getting what you need quickly, without stepping on toes.

Optimizing Scraping Speed

Speed isn't about hammering a website with requests. It's about reducing overhead, limiting redundant work, and making smart technical choices.

1. Limit What You Request

Don't download what you don't need:

- **Disable unnecessary resources**: If you're using a headless browser (like Selenium), block images, CSS, and fonts. You're after data, not design.
- **Use lightweight requests**: Stick to `requests.get()` instead of heavier tools when possible. Avoid browser automation unless you need it.

2. Reuse Connections

Use `requests.Session()` to keep a persistent connection across requests. This avoids the overhead of opening and closing TCP connections each time, speeding things up considerably.

```python
Edit
import requests
session = requests.Session()
response = session.get("https://example.com")
```

3. Cache What You Can

If the data doesn't change often, consider **caching responses** locally. Tools like `requests-cache` can help avoid re-downloading the same content.

Minimizing Server Load and Avoiding IP Blocking

Websites don't like being bombarded. If you overwhelm a server or look too much like a bot, expect a ban. Here's how to avoid trouble:

1. Use Delay and Throttling

Introduce a **random delay** between requests using `time.sleep()` with randomized intervals.

```python
Edit
import time, random
time.sleep(random.uniform(1, 3))   # Wait 1 to 3 seconds
```

2. Rotate User-Agents and IPs

A single IP sending too many requests too quickly? That's a red flag. You can avoid detection by:

- Rotating **User-Agent** headers to mimic different browsers
- Using **proxies** or services like ScraperAPI, BrightData, or residential proxy pools

```python
Edit
headers = {
    'User-Agent':
random.choice(user_agents_list)
}
```

244

3. Respect robots.txt and Site Structure

If a site explicitly says "don't scrape me" in its `robots.txt`, you're asking for problems by ignoring it. Also, avoid making concurrent requests to the same domain — spread your traffic out.

Efficient Data Extraction Strategies

Fast scraping isn't only about requests — how you **extract** and **process** the data matters too.

1. Use CSS Selectors Wisely

Instead of navigating a DOM tree step-by-step, use targeted CSS selectors to jump straight to the data.

```python
Edit
from bs4 import BeautifulSoup

soup = BeautifulSoup(html, "html.parser")
titles = soup.select("div.title > a")
```

2. Avoid Unnecessary Parsing

If you're only extracting JSON from a `<script>` tag, there's no need to parse the whole page with BeautifulSoup. Use regex or string matching instead when appropriate.

3. Batch Your Operations

Where possible, collect all the needed elements and process them in a single loop, rather than parsing the page over and over.

Real-World Example: Writing an Efficient Scraper That Minimizes Impact

Let's say you're scraping 500 pages of product listings from an online retailer. Here's how to do it cleanly:

- **Throttle Requests**: Add a randomized delay of 1–3 seconds between each page.
- **Use Sessions**: Maintain a persistent session using `requests.Session()` to reuse cookies and headers.
- **Avoid Redundant Requests**: Store visited URLs in a local cache or database so you don't revisit the same page.
- **Disable Images in Selenium** (if you have to use it):

```python
python
```

```
Edit
from     selenium.webdriver.chrome.options
import Options
options = Options()
prefs                                    =
{"profile.managed_default_content_setting
s.images": 2}
options.add_experimental_option("prefs",
prefs)
```

Results? The scraper completes in about 20 minutes, doesn't spike CPU or memory, and avoids triggering any anti-scraping measures.

Wrap-Up

Fast scrapers aren't reckless — they're smart. You get the data you need by reducing friction: fewer requests, lighter payloads, smarter parsing. Focus on being *quiet and efficient*. That way, you stay off radar, reduce your footprint, and make your scripts more sustainable.

In the next chapter, we'll wrap everything into a deployable solution — building a fully functional, production-ready web scraping application from scratch.

CHAPTER 26

TROUBLESHOOTING WEB

SCRAPING ISSUES

Web scraping seems straightforward... until it suddenly isn't. One day your scraper works. The next day it breaks. The problem could be a layout change, a CAPTCHA, a 403 error, or some unexpected nonsense in the data. If you're scraping at scale or on a schedule, debugging becomes a full-time habit.

This chapter is your troubleshooting handbook. We'll walk through real annoyances, what causes them, and how to fix or avoid them without tearing your hair out.

Common Scraping Problems and Their Solutions

Let's start with the stuff that breaks most scrapers:

1. HTML Changes Without Warning

Problem: Your code relies on specific HTML tags or class names that silently change.

Solution:

249

- Don't hardcode brittle selectors. Use broader or more stable identifiers.
- Re-inspect the page regularly and log what elements are found/missing.
- Use `try/except` to avoid crashes when an expected element is gone.

2. HTTP 403 or 401 Errors

Problem: You're getting blocked outright.

Solution:

- Rotate **user-agent headers** to mimic real browsers.
- Add **referrer headers**, cookies, and other headers to appear legitimate.
- Use a **proxy** if your IP has been blocked.

3. Empty or Incomplete Data

Problem: Your scraper returns blank fields or partial content.

Solution:

- Check if the data is loaded dynamically (JavaScript-rendered).
- Use Selenium or other tools to render the page fully.

- Scrape the network requests instead of the rendered HTML (check browser dev tools).

4. ReCaptcha or JavaScript Challenges

Problem: You're hit with a bot-check — CAPTCHA, Cloudflare checks, etc.

Solution:

- Headless browsers with human-like behavior can sometimes get through.
- For heavy CAPTCHA, either use CAPTCHA-solving services or pivot to API access.
- Reduce request frequency to avoid triggering rate limits.

Diagnosing Issues with Website Structure Changes

Most real-world scrapers break due to **frontend redesigns**. Here's how to spot and fix that:

1. Compare the Old and New HTML

If your script used to work, save a snapshot of the page. When things go sideways, compare it to the new source. You'll quickly spot changes in tags, classes, or element structure.

2. Log Everything

Add debug logs to your code that output:

- What URL was requested
- What status code was returned
- What elements were found
- What data was extracted

This helps you zero in on what went wrong, fast.

3. Use Fallbacks

Sometimes, one selector fails but another works. You can define backup logic:

```python
Edit
title = soup.select_one('.main-title') or
soup.select_one('h1.title')
```

Handling CAPTCHA, IP Bans, and Server Errors

When a site doesn't want you scraping it, it fights back. Here's how to handle it without a full-blown meltdown.

CAPTCHA

- If you only hit CAPTCHA occasionally, manually solve and reuse the session cookies.
- For large-scale scraping, use **anti-CAPTCHA services** (2Captcha, AntiCaptcha).
- Selenium with stealth plugins and proper delay patterns helps.

IP Bans

- Use **rotating proxy pools** (ScraperAPI, BrightData, or your own list).
- Respect rate limits — don't send 1000 requests in 2 minutes from one IP.
- Add **retry logic** with exponential backoff:

```python
Edit
for i in range(3):
    try:
        response = session.get(url)
        break
    except Exception:
        time.sleep(2 ** i)
```

Server Errors (500, 502, etc.)

- Don't retry instantly. Give the server time to recover.
- Monitor error rates and temporarily back off when things spike.

Real-World Example: Troubleshooting a Scraping Script

Let's say you built a scraper for a job listings site. It was working fine, then started returning empty job descriptions.

Steps to debug:

1. **Inspect the site manually** – Notice the job descriptions are now loaded via JavaScript.
2. **Look at the network tab** – Discover an XHR call fetching the data as JSON.
3. **Modify your scraper** – Switch from scraping the HTML to directly hitting the API endpoint.
4. **Problem solved** – You now pull clean JSON instead of parsing rendered HTML.

Always assume the site will change — and your scraper needs to be flexible, not fragile.

Wrap-Up

No scraper is future-proof, but that's not the goal. The key is building scripts that fail gracefully, tell you what's wrong, and are easy to tweak when the web moves the goalposts. Think of your scraper like plumbing — it needs maintenance, but if you build it right, you won't be calling the plumber every week.

Next up, we'll bring all the moving parts together into a full scraping application with everything you've learned — automation, storage, analysis, and resilience built in.

CHAPTER 27

FUTURE OF WEB SCRAPING AND CONCLUSION

You've made it to the final chapter. By now, you've gone from learning what scraping is to building scalable, resilient data pipelines. But web scraping isn't a fixed skill—it shifts constantly because the web shifts constantly. This chapter gives you a no-hype look at where things are headed, what might break your current tools, and how to stay sharp.

Trends and Future Challenges in Web Scraping

1. JavaScript-Heavy Websites Becoming the Norm

Static HTML is disappearing fast. More sites rely on frontend frameworks (React, Angular, Vue) that build the page on the client side. Traditional scraping methods like `requests` + `BeautifulSoup` can't see that content.

What that means for you:

- Headless browsers (Selenium, Playwright) and network traffic inspection will become standard tools.
- Scrapers that mimic real users will stay relevant longer.

2. Anti-Bot Defenses Are Getting Smarter

Sites are throwing everything at bots: CAPTCHAs, rate-limiting, IP blacklists, device fingerprinting. They can tell when you're not a human—even if your scraper acts polite.

What that means for you:

- You'll need stealth techniques (rotating proxies, fake browser headers, simulated mouse movement).
- Or just shift to APIs when available.

3. Legal Boundaries Are Tightening

Laws around scraping remain murky. While scraping public data isn't inherently illegal, violating terms of service or scraping personal information can land you in a lawsuit (or worse).

What that means for you:

- You'll have to weigh the usefulness of data against the legal and ethical risk.
- Respect `robots.txt` and TOS agreements.

Alternatives to Traditional Scraping

1. Web Scraping as a Service (WSaaS)

Tools like ScraperAPI, Octoparse, Apify, and ParseHub offer ready-to-go infrastructure:

- Built-in proxy rotation
- Captcha solving
- Browser emulation
- Visual point-and-click interfaces

They're not free, but they offload the technical headache. If you're scraping at scale or commercially, these services save a lot of time.

2. Direct API Access

If a site offers an API—**use it**. APIs are stable, predictable, and legally safer. They don't need parsing logic, are often faster, and require less maintenance.

3. Licensed Datasets

For news, social, and financial data, some companies now offer legally licensed datasets. If you're after reliability, this beats scraping live pages every time.

Conclusion and Final Thoughts

Web scraping is one of those skills that pays for itself—whether you're building dashboards, gathering leads, monitoring competitors, or fueling machine learning models. But it's not just about writing a scraper that works *once*. The real test is building something that works *again tomorrow*.

If there's one mindset you should leave this book with, it's this: **Treat the web like an unreliable friend. Be skeptical. Be defensive. Expect change.**

Keep your scrapers lean. Test often. Document everything. And most importantly, don't be lazy—when something breaks, figure out *why* instead of just trying random fixes. That's what separates a script hacker from someone who can run production-level data extraction pipelines.

Resources for Further Learning

Books

- *Web Scraping with Python* by Ryan Mitchell (O'Reilly)
- *Automate the Boring Stuff with Python* by Al Sweigart

Online Courses

- Real Python (realpython.com)
- Scrapy's official tutorials
- Udemy courses on BeautifulSoup, Selenium, and API integration

Communities and Forums

- r/webscraping on Reddit
- Stack Overflow (tagged `web-scraping`, `beautifulsoup`, `selenium`)
- Python Discord communities

Final note: If you're still here, congrats. Seriously. This stuff isn't flashy, but it gives you leverage most people don't have. Now go write something that pulls the data you want—and doesn't break when the site puts a `<div>` where a `<span>` used to be.